DATE DUE

		Discard	
GAYLORD			PRINTED IN U.S.A.

HUMAN
RIGHTS

HUMAN RIGHTS

Samuel Totten
and
Milton Kleg

ENSLOW PUBLISHERS, INC.

Bloy St. & Ramsey Ave. P.O. Box 38
Box 777   Aldershot
Hillside, N.J. 07205 Hants GU12 6BP
U.S.A.   U.K.

Library of Congress Cataloging-in-Publication Data

Totten, Samuel,
    Human rights / by Samuel Totten and Milton Kleg.
       p. cm.
    Includes bibliographies.
    Includes index.
    Summary: Describes the history of human rights and highlights
various violations of human rights, including discrimination,
racism, genocide, and torture.
    ISBN 0-89490-156-7
    1. Human rights. [1. Human rights.] I. Kleg, Milton.
II. Title.
JC599.U5T67 1988
323.4—dc19

                                  88-4257
                                    CIP
                                    AC

Printed in the United States of America

10 9 8 7 6 5 4 3 2

Photos courtesy of Amnesty International: pp. 44,79,124,132,140,145
147,156,209; **David Hawk:** pp. 113, 117; **Martin Luther King Center for
Social Change:** p.70; **National Archives:** 148-CCD-35, p.24/ 148-GW-662,
p. 27/ 16-N-6435, p.28/ 111-SC-95986, p.31/ 106-IN-205, p. 32/ 165-
WW-600A-2, p. 34/ 306-NT-650-2, p. 48/ 69-N-14838, p.55/ 306-NT-
15910C, p. 71/ 106-BAE-2517A, p. 74/ 111-SC-205613, p. 105/ 208-
AA-129G-11, p. 108; **United Nations Photo:** pp. 18,38,41,50,82,163,
197,221-227, UN/Contact, pp. 61,80,81, UN/W. A. Graham, p. 184,
UN/Paul Heath Hoeffel, p. 198, UN/A. Holbrooks, p. 206, UN/John
Isaac, pp. 166,171,176,188, UN/Peter Magubane, pp. 15,181, UN/O.
Monson, p. 201, UN/W. Raynore, p. 63, UN/Kate Truscott, p. 212, UN/L.
Van Esscne, p. 12; **Zoryan Institute:** pp. 97,100.

To five outstanding and compassionate educators who have displayed, through their words and actions, their vital concern for the protection of human rights:

> Israel Charny
> Maxine Greene
> Robert Hitchcock
> Charles Rivera
> John Anthony Scott
>
> —Samuel Totten

To Anna, Joel, Rachel, Esther, Devorah, and Itamar.
> —Milton Kleg

Contents

Acknowledgments

I wish to thank Dr. Israel Charny, Professor Drew Christie, Jean Craven, Scott Harrison, Ellen Moore, Charles Rivera, and Michael Totten for their many astute editorial suggestions.

Gratitude is also gladly extended to the following persons for the time and assistance they gave in providing us with many of the photographs found in this book: Alison Cattermole, Betsy Ross, Suzannah Sirkin, and Emily Troutmann of Amnesty International USA; Monica Butler and D. Williams at the United Nations Photo Library; and David Hawk.

—Samuel Totten

I should like to thank Bruce Henard of Boulder, Colorado, for his suggestions, criticisms, and patience. Bruce literally sat over my shoulder as I toiled through the chapters on racism and hunger. Appreciation is also extended to Dr. Robert Wershaw for his review and comments regarding the chapter on hunger.

—Milton Kleg

"If we cannot be concerned about human rights abroad, we are less likely to be concerned about human rights at home."

—Melvin Maddocks, journalist

1

Introducing Human Rights

What Are Human Rights?

It is 1963. In Washington, D.C., standing in front of the Lincoln Memorial, the Reverend Dr. Martin Luther King, Jr., looks out over the throngs of thousands of people—over two hundred thousand. There are people of all races and religions, the rich and the poor, men, women, and children from throughout the United States. Some are holding signs reading WE MARCH FOR FIRST CLASS CITIZENSHIP NOW and WE DEMAND VOTING RIGHTS NOW. Another sign reads CIVIL RIGHTS PLUS FULL EMPLOYMENT EQUALS FREEDOM. Others hold pennants which simply read, WE SHALL OVERCOME. As a hot August sun beats down, a hush comes over the crowd.

"I'm happy to join with you today in what will go down in history as the greatest demonstration for freedom in the history of our nation." With these opening words, Dr. King begins what has been called one of the most stirring speeches in the history of the American civil rights movement.

He continues: "I have a dream that one day on the red hills of Georgia the sons of former slaves and the sons of former slaveowners will be able to sit down together at the table of brotherhood. . . .

I have a dream that my four little children will one day live in a nation where they will not be judged by the color of their skin but by the content of their character. . . ."

As Dr. King concludes his address, he raises his right arm as if to plead to a greater power for all peoples: "Let freedom ring. . . ." His voice rises, and the words echo strongly over the many loudspeakers.

"When we allow freedom to ring, when we let it ring from every village and every hamlet, from every state and every city, we will be able to speed up the day when all of God's children, black men and white men, Jews and Gentiles, Protestants and Catholics, will be able to join hands and sing in the words of the old Negro spiritual, 'Free at last! Free at last! Thank God Almighty, we are free at last!'"

For Dr. King and millions of others in America and throughout the world, "Free at last" means having rights— human rights. These are the rights that enable people to become what they choose to become, to have their own beliefs, to have equal respect and dignity. It means being able to love and grow, to learn and share, to be at peace with themselves and their fellow human beings.

For many, the dream has made much progress in becoming a reality. For others, it is still a dream. For Ana María Martínez, it is a dream that she will never experience.

A young Argentine woman, Ana María was expecting her first child. While walking about half a block from her home in a suburb of Buenos Aires, a Ford Falcon pulled up alongside of Ana. The car was the same kind that was used by the secret police of Argentina. At gunpoint, Ana was forced into the car.

Two weeks later, Ana María was found slain. She lay half buried along a riverbank. It is believed that Ana María Martínez was murdered because she had chosen to belong to a political party that was opposed by the Argentine government. For Ana María Martínez and her unborn child, the dream was shattered and ended.

Her death was not a rare incident in Argentina between 1976 and the early 1980s. During this time, over six thousand Argentines, young children and babies as well as adults, mysteriously disappeared or were killed. Some people were killed in torture chambers and then dumped into rivers; others were flown in planes over the Atlantic Ocean and pushed out to drown.

There are approximately two hundred nations in the world, and human rights organizations report that dozens and dozens of countries have, at various times and for various reasons, either mistreated, abused, or killed their citizens. When a country treats its citizens in any of these ways, it is depriving them of their basic human rights. Such a situation is commonly referred to as "the deprivation of human rights."

On May 8, 1986, twelve East German army reserve soldiers tried to blast their way through a subway tunnel in order to reach freedom on the other side of the Berlin Wall. Their attempt, however, was stopped when regular East German guards, who were the reserve soldiers' fellow countrymen, shot and killed at least six of the soldiers. The others were captured and immediately executed.

The East Germans built the Berlin Wall in the summer of 1961 in order to divide the city of Berlin permanently in two and to prevent the East German citizens from fleeing to a freer way of life. Since that time, however, over twenty-five thousand people have escaped over it or through its barricades. Many others have been killed in their attempt to do so.

East Germany is not the only country that attempts to prevent its people from moving somewhere else when they desire to do so. This primarily happens in countries that are totalitarian (those nations whose governments maintain almost complete control over their citizens).

Archbishop Desmond Tutu, winner of the 1984 Nobel Peace Prize, is greatly respected around the world for being a man of peace. In his own country of South Africa, though, he is not allowed to vote, run for political office, live in certain neighborhoods, or shop in certain stores. Why? Because he is black.

South Africa is just one example of a country where people are treated unfairly simply because of their race or religion. Again, such incidents are classic examples of human rights violations.

A squatter settlement in South Africa is shown.

It seems natural that most people would not like to be told what they can or cannot say or write or where they can or cannot live or shop. And surely, most people also would not want to live under a government that jails, tortures, or kills its citizens for disagreeing with some of its policies or for belonging to a political or religious group that the leaders do not trust.

But many people continue to be mistreated, imprisoned, or killed by their governments for these very reasons. Almost every week there is at least one article in the newspaper or report on television about someone (or a group of people) who has been unfairly punished or deprived of his or her basic human rights.

However, as both politicians and educators frequently point out, many people (children and adults) who live in democratic countries such as the United States rarely take the time to stop and think about how unfair or unhappy the lives of some people are. They seldom give much thought as to how precious their own freedom and rights are to them, or how lucky they are to live in a nation where human rights and justice are, for the most part, guaranteed and protected.

But as a former prisoner of conscience (a person who is arrested because of either his or her beliefs, color, ethnic origin, or religion) once said: "Before the nightmare of being locked up and tortured I rarely, if ever, thought about how much I valued my freedom. But during my imprisonment, that's all I thought about. And that, as I see it, is part of the problem in our world—too many people do not really value what they have until it is taken away. Then, though, it is often too late."

The term "human rights" has been mentioned several times, but what exactly are "human rights"? Ordinary "rights" are different from "human rights." Some "rights" are given to people, while others are earned or purchased.

For instance, a hunter may be given the right to cross some-body's private land in order to hunt. Or, by winning a political election, a person earns the right to serve as a member of the government. And when a person buys land he or she has gained the right to use that land.

"Human rights" are not given to someone out of kindness or love, and one does not have to earn them. Every person is entitled to them simply because he or she is human. Human rights are rights that come with birth. Because of that, human rights are universal. These rights apply to all people through-out the world regardless of their nationality, race, religion, political beliefs, age, or sex.

In today's world many different types of human rights are generally acknowledged to be basic rights. These include civil, political, economic, social, and cultural rights. Chapter 2 will discuss the history behind these rights as well as present more information on what makes up such rights.

Basically the civil and political rights include the right to life, liberty, political participation, freedom of expression, and freedom from torture and slavery, as well as many others. Economic, social, and cultural rights are concerned with such issues as the right to work, to have "a standard of living ade-quate for the health and well-being of a family, including food, clothing, housing and medical care . . ."; an education; and the right to "enjoy the arts and to share in scientific ad-vancement and its benefits." These and other rights are listed in the Universal Declaration of Human Rights beginning on page 221.

While there has been a growing concern regarding the guarantee and protection of more and more people's human rights, many human rights activists believe that there is still a long way to go before one can sit back and be satisfied with the current situation. That is true because far too many

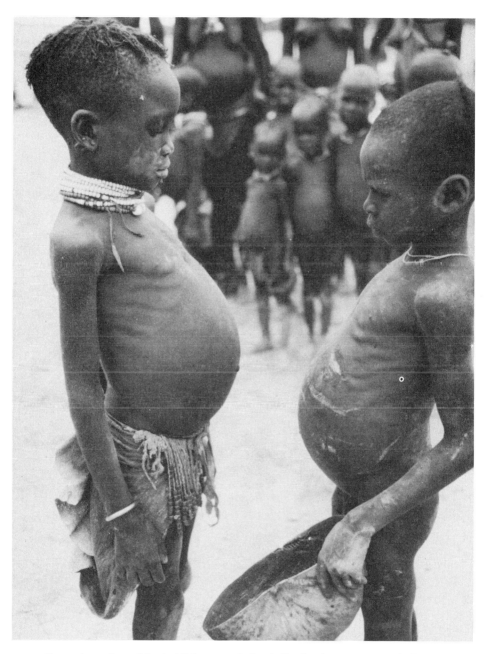

Severely malnourished children await food distribution at a camp in Bumi, Ethiopia.

people—people like Ana María Martínez, the East German soldiers, and Archbishop Tutu—suffer injustices at the hands of their governments.

Why do these situations exist? Undoubtedly there are many reasons. However, even partially to begin to understand the main ones, a person needs to know something about the history of human rights.

"One thing I believe profoundly: We make our own history. The course of history is directed by the choices we make and our own choices grow out of the ideas, the beliefs, the values, the dreams of the people."

—Eleanor Roosevelt, human rights activist

2

The History of Human Rights

DACHAU CAPTURED BY AMERICANS WHO KILL GUARDS, LIBERATE 32,000

Dachau, Germany, April 30, 1945 [*The New York Times*] Dachau, Germany's most dreaded extermination camp, has been captured and its surviving 32,000 tortured inmates have been freed by outraged American troops. . . .

Dashing to the camp atop tanks, bulldozers—anything with wheels—the [soldiers] hit the notorious prison soon after lunch yesterday.

. . . Bodies were found in many places. Here also were the gas chambers—camouflaged as "showers" into which prisoners were herded thinking they were going to bathe—and the cremation ovens. Huge stacks of clothing bore mute testimony to the fate of their owners.

The main part of the camp is surrounded by a fifteen foot moat through which a torrent of water circulates. Atop a ten foot fence is charged barbed wire.

Inside the barracks were more than 1,000 bodies—some shot by guards, others victims of disease and starvation.

The atrocities that were committed in Dachau and the other Nazi death camps during the early 1940s led many nations to vote in favor of developing and abiding by the Universal Declaration of Human Rights. The officials of such

Two South African children are seemingly unaware of racial discrimination in their nation.

18

governments felt that something dramatic and important had to be done to tell the world that everyone was entitled to basic human rights and that every country was obligated to protect such rights. Since 1948, the year in which the declaration was established, it has been cited time and again as a major step on the long road toward guaranteeing the human rights of all people.

In order to understand the full significance that the declaration has for humanity, as well as to understand why abuses of human rights still occur on a regular basis, a person needs to know how the people of the past looked upon human rights.

Ancient Societies and Human Rights

Many ancient societies—among them the ancient Jewish, Greek, and the Chinese—had rules and laws that were concerned with the human rights of certain peoples in their society. The key point here is that while some people enjoyed rights, others did not.

It has been claimed by some scholars that the Ten Commandments of the ancient Jews is one of the earliest human rights documents. Indeed, according to the Jews there are seven commandments that apply to all peoples. Among those that are closest to today's human rights concerns are "Thou shalt not murder," and "All nations must appoint judges and have courts of justice." The Ten Commandments along with 603 other laws determined how the Jewish state was to be governed. Historians have also pointed out that by A.D. 1200 many of the leading Christian scholars regarded the commandments as part of a universal natural law that governed human conduct.

In the early days of the Greek city-states, citizens were entitled to what was called *isonomia,* or equality before the law. That simply meant that the laws of the land would apply

19

to every citizen in the same way. The Greek city-state citizens were also allowed the right of *isogoria,* or freedom of speech.

In the ancient Greek city–states, however, all of the people were divided into three main classes or categories. Athens had the following groups: citizens, who were the most numerous, slaves, and resident aliens (or noncitizens). In Sparta there were the citizens, serfs (servants or slaves), and resident aliens.

Those people who were citizens had the most rights. But even among citizens there were those who were treated better and had more rights than others. On the other hand, while serfs could own property in Sparta, they were not allowed to move from the place where they had been born. While noncitizens in both Athens and Sparta enjoyed personal freedom, they didn't have any political rights such as the privilege to vote and hold political office. Except for certain brief periods during these early years, women did not have political rights in the city–states.

Later in Greek history, during the Hellenistic period, some philosophers began to claim that all people—regardless of one's position in society—should be guaranteed certain political and human rights. This was a great change in attitude from past practice. It was such an important change that these philosophers are said to be responsible for starting the discussions and debates that have gone on for centuries about the meaning and significance of human rights for the "common person."

In another part of the world around 200 B.C. many Chinese began to live by the idea that is expressed in the Golden Rule—"Do unto others as you would have them do unto you." The rule is called golden to show that it is the best and highest rule of life. Throughout history, many other groups of people have also attempted to live by the Golden Rule—including people who were Christian and Jewish.

During part of its history the ancient Chinese also employed people to serve as censors of the government. A censor is one who supervises such concerns as morals and conduct. These censors were scholars who studied or taught the teachings of the philosopher named Confucius. It was their job to oversee, and criticize, if necessary, the emperor and his officials when they mistreated people or did not follow the laws in a fair way.

The Middle Ages and Human Rights

As time went on, more nations and empires established laws to protect the human rights of their citizens; however, as in ancient Greece, these laws often did not apply to the slaves, serfs, peasants, women, or foreigners in society. Also, as some nations or empires crumbled and disappeared, so did the laws that protected the people's human rights.

An example of this situation was when the Roman Empire gradually fell apart and was divided into many kingdoms. This was during the time from about A.D. 350 to A.D. 1450, a period called the Middle Ages. In the Roman Empire, citizens had been provided with safety and security through the various laws that were in place. However, when the so-called barbarians took over, law and order was replaced by much harsher forms of justice.

An example of one form of this sort of justice was "trial by ordeal." During a trial by ordeal a person who was suspected of a crime was forced to shove his arm into a bucket of boiling water or to grab a burning hot iron with his bare hand. If the burns from these tortures healed within a period of three days, the person was declared innocent. If the wounds did not heal within that time then he or she was declared guilty, and hanged. Not only were these forms of torture extremely painful, but they often ensured a guilty verdict since such burns rarely healed in three days' time.

That was not the only type of torture that people were made to suffer during the Middle Ages in Europe. During the major part of the Middle Ages most people considered Christianity to be the only "true" religion, and regarded the Catholic Church as the only "true" Church. If a person refused to believe in the teachings of the Church then he or she was often called a heretic. Heretics were regularly tortured and/or killed. They were beaten with sticks, had their feet slowly roasted on burning coals, and were burned to death.

The Magna Carta and the English Bill of Rights
In England toward the end of the Middle Ages, the wealthy landowners or barons stood up against the suffering they were subject to under the rule of King John. In 1215, they forced him to place his seal on a document called the Magna Carta, which means "great charter" in Latin.

The purpose of the Magna Carta was to force the king to rule in a fair manner and to protect the barons from unfair treatment by the government. Even though ordinary freemen and peasants made up the largest portion of England's population at this time, they were barely mentioned in the Magna Carta. As a result, the Magna Carta was not greeted with much enthusiasm by the average person. However, as time passed many of the rights and guarantees granted to the barons were extended to the common people.

For example, the thirty-ninth article of the Magna Carta originally guaranteed trial by jury for only barons and freemen. Later, this right was interpreted as applying to all persons. The spirit of the Magna Carta, that is the idea of guaranteeing the basic rights of people, outlived the specific details mentioned in the document. As a result, even the common people began to think of the Magna Carta as a basic guarantee of their rights. Today, the Magna Carta is hailed as one of the most important landmarks in the history of human rights and free government.

Nevertheless, just because the Magna Carta was written up and agreed upon, it did not automatically guarantee that all of the rights outlined in it would be honored or carefully followed by all of the monarchs who came after King John. And the fact of the matter is, not all of the rights spelled out in the Magna Carta were honored. This greatly angered the barons as well as the ordinary freemen and peasants, and in the 1600s they decided that they were no longer going to put up with such poor treatment and began to rebel.

One of the Englishmen's main concerns was that many people were being arrested and thrown in jail for long periods of time (up to several years) before their guilt or innocence was even established. Put another way, a person in those days who had not committed any crime often spent more time in jail than people do today who have been found guilty of a crime.

By rebelling, the Englishmen were basically telling the king this: "Look, the Magna Carta guarantees that a person will be treated fairly if arrested, but that is not happening." After many heated political battles, the principle of habeas corpus was developed. The basic idea behind this principle is that anyone who is arrested has the right to a speedy trial as well as immediate release from jail if found innocent.

The fight carried on by those Englishmen back in the 1600s also resulted in two more very significant human rights documents; the Petition of Right of 1628 and the English Bill of Rights of 1689. Both of these put limits on the king's power and gave more power to the Parliament and the courts. By doing so, the English people hoped to be treated more fairly.

The English Bill of Rights had a profound impact on how leaders and people in other nations began to view the concept of human rights. With its emphasis on both political and civil rights, it came to serve as a model of human rights legislation for other Western nations. As Voltaire, the French writer, pointed out: "English law has restored each man to all the rights of nature of which he has been deprived in most monarchies. These rights are: full liberty of his person [and] of his goods; freedom to speak to the nation by the pen; freedom not to be tried under any criminal charge except by a jury formed of independent men; freedom not to be tried in any case except according to the precise terms of the law; freedom to profess peacefully any religion he wishes."

The second Continental Congress voting for independence from Britain is depicted in this painting by Robert Pine and Edward Savage.

The Declaration of Independence and U.S. Bill of Rights

Ironically, the English Bill of Rights had a tremendous effect on the colonists in America. As you probably recall, one of the main reasons early settlers fled from England to the New World was to escape religious persecution. For example, a Puritan who published a pamphlet in England proposing reforms in the Church of England was fined, jailed, whipped, and had his forehead burned with a red-hot iron.

As time went on, however, those in the New World found themselves constantly under the thumb of England. The colonists not only believed that they were being unfairly taxed by the king, but were even angrier that in light of the high taxes they paid, the English government still refused to allow the colonists to have a say in how their colony was to be governed. The colonists claimed that it was unfair to be subjected to "taxation without representation."

Greatly embittered over this treatment and inspired by the establishment of the English Bill of Rights, the colonists finally decided to declare their own independence from England. In Philadelphia on Thursday evening, July 4, 1776, the colonists published the "Declaration of Independence." In that document it is stated that "We hold these Truths to be self-evident, that all Men are created equal, that they are endowed by their Creator with certain unalienable Rights, that among these are Life, Liberty and the Pursuit of Happiness."

In declaring their independence from England, the colonists claimed that the rights guaranteed in the English Bill of Rights were universal rights—the rights of all men, not just Englishmen. The idea of "universal rights" was based on the concept of "natural rights." More specifically, philosopher John Locke had earlier claimed that certain rights—like the right to life, liberty, and property—are derived from the laws of nature. In that sense, every person is naturally entitled to them. Over time, other rights that came to be perceived by modern man as natural, like economic rights, were gradually added to this list.

Following the bitter war between the revolutionaries and the English, the United States of America was founded. After much heated discussion and debate during which time as many as seventeen constitutions were drawn up, the Founding Fathers settled upon the United States Constitution of 1787. To this was added the Bill of Rights in 1789. Although the Constitution has been criticized for its recognition of slavery and not accepting the American Indian on an equal basis, it is considered along with the Bill of Rights by many scholars to be among the great documents of free government. It was one of the few times in history that a government was given its authority to rule by the people. To this day, many people around the world look upon the United States and its Constitution as the hallmarks of freedom.

Not All People Were Treated Equally

Just as the Magna Carta did not assure complete freedom and justice for every member of England's society, neither did the U.S. Constitution or the Bill of Rights in American society. For numerous years black people, Indians, and women were (and to a certain extent, continue to be) treated like second-class citizens or worse in the United States. How so?

First of all, even as the U.S. Constitution and Bill of Rights were being drawn up, black people led a life of slavery. As a matter of fact, many of the Founding Fathers of the United States of America—the same ones who had declared that "all men are created equal"—owned slaves. A primary reason for this contradictory behavior is that at this time in history in the United States, black people were incorrectly seen by many whites as uncivilized and, in some cases, as less than human.

26

The type of life a slave led depended upon the master or owner he or she had. Some slaves were treated very well, while others were treated in a brutal manner. Quite often they had to do extremely hard, backbreaking work.

Those slaves whose owners or overseers were cruel led very miserable lives. They were often not given enough to eat nor enough warm clothes to wear. Also, in extreme situations slaves sometimes had their ears cut off for listening to a white person's conversation or their hands cut off for stealing.

A former slave, Henry Johnson, long ago told about the

The signing of the Declaration of Independence is depicted in this painting by John Trumbull.

harsh way in which many slaves were treated by their masters or overseers:

> I had to take a little hoe and dig weeds out of de crop. If our white boss see a little grasse we overlooked he would handcuff our feet to a whipping post, den chain de slave around de stomach to de post and strape de chin over de post and place your hands in front of you.
>
> Slaves have been stripped naked and lashed, often to death. Dey would be left strapped after from twenty-five to fifty lashes. . . . De next day, de overseer would be back with a heavy paddle full of holes dat had been dipped in boiling water and beat until de whole body was full of blisters. Den he'd take a cat-and-nine-tails dipped in hot salt water to draw out de bruised blood and would open every of dem blisters with dat. If de slave did not die from dat torture, he would be unfastened from de whipping post, and made to go to de field just as he was. Oftentimes he would die shortly after. Dey did de same to women.

This store is for blacks only in Belle Glade, Florida, 1945.

Another slave, Julia Brown, has also told about how members of slave families were often forcibly separated from one another, and sold like livestock:

> Slaves were treated in most cases like cattle. A man went about the country buyin' up slaves like buyin' up cattle and the like, and he was called a "speculator." Then he'd sell 'em to the highest bidder. Oh! it was pitiful to see chillen taken from their mothers' breasts, mothers sold, husbands sold from wives. One woman he was to buy had a baby . . ., and he wouldn't want the baby, said he hadn't bargained to buy the baby, and he just wouldn't.

Of course, not all slaves were treated in this way. Some were permitted to be educated and were well treated. But the point is that they were not free, and their fate was in the hands of a master who could do with the slave as he or she wished.

It was not until almost a hundred years after the founding of the nation that black people were freed from such bondage. That was in 1863, following the Emancipation Proclamation. Even then, though, black people did not enjoy the same freedom and rights of white people. Almost another century passed before every state in the nation would accept the rights of black people to attend the same schools and live in the same neighborhoods as whites, use the same water fountains and rest rooms as whites, eat in the same restaurants and shop in the same stores as whites, and compete for the same jobs on an equal basis with whites.

American Indians, who lived in America long before the arrival of the white man, were also ill-treated, off and on for hundreds of years by the U.S. government. In the 1800s the government sent troops to forcibly take the Indians' land from them. During this time many Indians were slaughtered by

U.S. troops. One man, Robert Bent, witnessed the slaughter of the Cheyennes in 1864:

> I saw the American flag waving [in the Cheyenne's camp] and heard Black Kettle tell the Indians to stand around the flag, and there they were huddled—men, women, and children. This was when we [the troops] were fifty yards from the Indians. I also saw a white flag raised. . . . When the troops fired, the Indians ran, probably to get their arms. Everyone I saw dead was scalped by the troops. I saw quite a number of infants in the arms of their mothers killed.

Other Indians, who reluctantly agreed to give up their land, were often forced onto reservations comprised of dry and useless land hundreds of miles from their original homes. In some cases, when the U.S. government decided that the Indians' new land was valuable, it again forced the Indians to move. In response to this sort of treatment, one chief said: "I think the Great White Father [the president of the United States] had better put the Indians on wheels and then you can run them [the Indians] about whenever you want."

Speaking of these different situations, Chief Joseph, leader of the Nez Percé Indians, had this to say in 1877:

> I do not understand why nothing is done for my people. I have heard talk and talk, but nothing is done. Words do not pay for my dead people. They do not pay for my country, now overrun by white men. . . . They do not give me back my children. . . . If the white man wants to live in peace with the Indians he can live in peace. There need be no trouble. Treat all men alike. Give them all the same law. All men were made by the same Great Spirit Chief. They are all brothers. The earth is mother of all people, and all people should have equal rights.

A treaty is signed by William T. Sherman and the Sioux Indians at Fort
Laramie, Wyoming, 1868.

Joseph (Himaton-Yalakit) was the chief of the Nez Percé Indians.

I only ask of the government to be treated as all other men are treated. . . . We ask to be recognized as men.

Let me be a free man—free to travel, free to stop, free to work, free to trade where I choose, free to choose my own teachers, free to follow the religion of my fathers, free to think and talk and act for myself—and I will obey every law, or submit to the penalty.

The Native Americans, however, would not receive such freedom for a long time. They were not given the right to vote until 1924, almost one hundred and forty years after the ratification of the U.S. Constitution. Even to this day, Native Americans are fighting in court to regain the land rights that their ancestors had stolen from them by the government.

Throughout a large part of U.S. history, women have also been treated as less than equal to men. For instance, they were not allowed to vote until 1920. Furthermore, for many years, including late into the twentieth century, women were strongly discouraged from entering politics, and were flatly denied the right to work at many jobs of their choice.

For over sixty years various groups of women, along with many men, have tried to make the Equal Rights Amendment (ERA) part of the Constitution. Simply stated, the ERA would guarantee that by law men and women would be treated equally. Although the U.S. House of Representatives voted in favor of the ERA 354-13 and the U.S. Senate 84-8, it was not ratified by enough states by the 1982 deadline. Thus, it did not become part of the Constitution.

The ERA has been a very controversial issue. There are many men and women who are against it for various reasons. One of the most outspoken critics of the amendment is Phyllis Schlafly, and she has said, "The truth is that American women have never had it so good. Why should we lower ourselves to 'equal rights' when we already have the status of

Suffragists picket the White House in 1917. Sixteen of the women were jailed for two days.

special privilege?" Plenty of women, however, disagree with her and feel that the Equal Rights Amendment is needed if women are going to enjoy the same rights as men in U.S. society.

All of the above mentioned problems that blacks, Native Americans and women have faced in the United States have been mentioned in order to point out that even in the United States—which is widely acknowledged as the "land of the free"—many different people have not always automatically had their human rights honored and protected. On the other hand, while some groups and individuals still suffer from prejudice and unequal treatment or poverty in the United States, many people believe that the nation is continuing to make great strides in trying to honor and protect the human rights of all citizens.

France's Declaration of the Rights of Man
Going back in time, it is worth noting that after the colonists' call for freedom and the American Revolution, the French people also began insisting on guaranteed human rights. Both the poor and middle-class people in French society rebelled at this time for various reasons. While the nobles were wealthy and lived lives of luxury, many peasants often did not have enough to eat. Also, while the nobles and members of the clergy did not have to pay taxes, the middle and lower classes had to pay huge amounts of tax. Finally, many people in the middle class also felt that the king should not have as much power over their lives as he did.

In July of 1789, the middle class and peasant people rebelled and overthrew the nobles and king. Following a bloody battle, the French issued a document called the Declaration of the Rights of Man and Citizen. That eventually resulted in a French constitution that provided the rights that the French people had been demanding.

Throughout the nineteenth and twentieth centuries, other nations—initially across Europe, and then later in Asia, Latin America, and Africa—followed the lead of the United States and France by adopting constitutions that included a section on basic human rights. However, as we have seen, adopting such constitutions and honoring them are two very different matters.

Up through the 1940s it was up to each country to protect its citizens' rights. At the same time, not much at all was being done to put pressure on those countries that were depriving citizens of their human rights.

Universal Declaration of Human Rights
That situation dramatically changed after the world was shocked by the discovery that the Nazis had slaughtered six million Jewish people during the years 1938 through 1945. It was in 1945, as World War II came to a close and the United States and British troops freed the survivors from the Nazis' concentration and death camps, that photographs and stories of the atrocities that had taken place were seen and heard around the world.

It was then that many people in the world realized that the protection of human rights was not simply the concern of individual nations, but that it needed to be the concern of all humanity. They came to believe that if one country's soldiers or police were killing or torturing their citizens then other countries should not stand by and ignore the situation. Instead, they had to say or do something about it. These people were basically saying what Vladimir Hertzog, a Brazilian journalist who was later possibly tortured to death in a Brazilian jail, once said prior to his death: "If we lose our ability to be outraged when we see others being tortured and killed, then we lose our right to call ourselves civilized human beings."

At the end of World War II the United Nations (UN) was founded through the UN Charter. Made up of nations from around the world, the UN's main purpose was to try to bring about and maintain world peace. Many of the members of the UN strongly believed that if a nation did not protect its citizens' human rights then there was a good chance that peace could not be maintained. Why? Because there would always be the possibility that those who were being denied their rights would rebel, which could result in a civil war or revolution.

Out of the above-mentioned concern and also over the great concern about the atrocities committed by the Nazis, the UN immediately went to work on the "internationalization" of human rights. It attempted to "internationalize" human rights by listing all those rights that every single person in the world—regardless of one's nationality, race, religion, sex, or profession—was entitled to as a human being. At the same time, by internationalizing human rights, the UN was taking the stance that from now on, the issue of guaranteeing and protecting a person's human rights would no longer simply be the business of individual nations, but of all nations. That meant that if one nation began to abuse its people's human rights then it was the duty of other nations to do everything they could to halt the abuse as soon as possible.

In 1945, through its charter, the UN made a general declaration that no one in the world should be discriminated against because of race, religion, language, or sex. Three years later, on Friday, December 10, 1948, the UN General Assembly voted in favor of establishing the Universal Declaration of Human Rights. The declaration was the first document in the history of humanity to state that every person on earth was entitled to both political and civil as well as economic, social, and cultural rights. But what, exactly, are those rights?

37

Political and civil rights include the right to life, liberty, and the freedom of expression. These are set out in order to make sure that a government treats its citizens in a fair and just manner. These have long been called "traditional" human rights. That is because there has been a long tradition in which people have both claimed and fought for such rights.

Economic, social, and cultural rights are such as the right to food, housing, health care, and an education. The establishment of these rights basically told governments that they have a responsibility to make sure that their citizens lead a decent life. These rights only gained wide recognition as "basic human rights" when they were declared to be such in the Universal Declaration.

Eleanor Roosevelt examines the Universal Declaration of Human Rights document she helped to develop.

The Universal Declaration has been repeatedly hailed as a landmark document in the area of human rights for two main reasons: one, it included the new and very significant components of economic, social, and cultural rights, and two, it "internationalized" concern for human rights.

The Controversy Surrounding the Declaration
There was a lot of disagreement among different nations as to which rights should be included in the declaration. For instance, James P. Hendrick, a U.S. State Department employee in 1945, said that the Soviet Union stressed the need to include all sorts of economic and social rights but felt that "the less said about freedom of speech, the rights to a fair trial, etc., the better." The United States, however, did not agree. It felt that if those political and civil rights were not included in the declaration then it would be next to useless.

Also, when the Soviet Union argued in favor of an economic right that guaranteed full employment for every citizen, the United States said it was willing to "promote" full employment, but not guarantee it. For this reason, as well as others, the Soviet Union did not cast a vote, either in favor or against, the declaration.

Attempting to explain the position of the United States, Eleanor Roosevelt, the U.S. representative on the UN Human Rights Commission, told the Soviet Union that "A society in which everyone works is not necessarily a free society and may indeed be a slave society; on the other hand, a society in which there is widespread economic insecurity can turn freedom into a barren and lifeless right for millions of people." In effect, she was saying that both a free society and one in which people had a place to live and enough to eat were equally important.

White Southerners in the U.S. Congress also had second

thoughts about supporting any document that outlawed discrimination or the unequal treatment of one group toward another group. They felt this way because most of the white citizens in their states wanted to maintain their power over the black people to keep the blacks in the position of second-class citizens.

Four Moslem nations also did not cast a vote either for or against the Universal Declaration. They believed that the right concerning religious freedom went against their holy book called the Koran. The Koran states that there is only one true religion that Muslims can believe in, and that is Islam.

Finally, South Africa also did not cast a vote. Eleanor Roosevelt reported that the delegate from South Africa said the country "hoped to give its people basic human rights, but that the Declaration went too far." Many South African whites apparently felt this way because they wanted to keep their black population in an inferior position to themselves.

Teams of UN members were later organized in order to set up specific lists of human rights, and these were called covenants or written, binding agreements. Basically, these were a list of rights that governments around the world agreed to guarantee and protect. It was not until 1966 that the first two covenants—the International Covenant on Economic, Social, and Cultural Rights and the International Covenant on Civil and Political Rights—were adopted by the UN General Assembly. However, it took another ten years (1976) before enough UN member nations had ratified (formally approved) the covenants in order to make them official.

The Value of the Universal Declaration and UN Covenants
Many people wonder whether the Universal Declaration of Human Rights and the Covenants have really helped to pro-

tect the rights of people around the globe. The answer is both yes and no.

These documents have certainly helped to make the issue of human rights a worldwide concern. That concern alone has brought about many important changes.

First, those nations that are members of the United Nations know that they are being watched by the UN and that they are expected to both protect their citizens and not deprive them of their human rights. In many cases this has actually brought about positive results. Second, it has encouraged recently formed nations to develop and adopt constitutions

Children play outside their tin shanty house where they and their families are forced to live in Cape Town, South Africa.

that include bills of rights that guarantee their citizens the rights outlined in the Universal Declaration. Over the long haul of history such a situation has been a rare event. Third, it has resulted in the establishment of numerous human rights organizations whose main purposes have been to put pressure on nations not to abuse their citizens' human rights and to educate the general public about human rights. All of these situations have made more people aware of the role and importance of human rights than ever before.

Why, then, is the answer also no? The major problem is that different governments in different parts of the world value or place greater emphasis on certain rights more than others. As a result, those rights that governments do not value as much often are not protected the way they should.

For instance, in the democratic nations of Europe and North America, political and civil rights and freedoms such as voting, a speedy and fair trial, freedom of speech and movement, and so on, are considered highly important. Some critics, however, contend that some of these nations place much less value on economic rights such as making sure that all of their citizens have a place to live, enough to eat, and good health care. For instance, in June of 1987 *Time* magazine reported that in Los Angeles, California, alone, over thirty thousand people live on the street because they cannot afford to rent or buy an apartment or house. Up to two hundred thousand poor people, it said, are forced to live in "garages, automobiles, even tool sheds and converted chicken coops."

Communist governments, on the other hand, place a much higher priority on such economic and social rights as the right to have enough food, full employment, and adequate housing and health care. But they do not place such a high priority on political and civil rights. As a result of this, while most of their citizens have jobs, enough to eat, and a place to

42

live, many are not able to speak freely, write what they wish, travel where they want, vote, or practice the religion of their choice.

The situation in the Third World (poor, undeveloped, or developing) nations varies from nation to nation. While some of them strive to protect the political rights of their citizens, others deny their citizens such rights. The latter situation exists for at least two main reasons. First, many of these nations, as found in Africa, were colonies under foreign rule well into the 1900s. Under foreign rule individual freedom was almost unheard of until very recently. It was not a tradition as it has been in Europe and North America. Second, since the people in the poor nations often do not have enough food to eat or clothes to wear or places to live, their leaders often insist that economic rights need to be met before the political rights are guaranteed. There is a great controversy over this point of view in that most of the citizens in these countries believe that they should immediately receive both the political and civil rights as well as the economic and social rights.

There are still other important reasons why human rights abuses take place. Some governments and nations are run by certain groups of people who distrust, dislike, or hate people who are different from themselves. This was true in Germany during the 1930s and 1940s when the Nazis hated and attempted to annihilate the Jewish people. It is also true today. In South Africa, for instance, the white-run government denies black people their basic rights. Also, in Iran the fundamentalist (a very strict following of a religion and its beliefs) Muslims have tortured and killed hundreds of peaceful people simply because they practice the Bahá'í religion.

Another motive of governments to deny freedoms and rights is their fear of being overthrown. In many cases this fear may be justified, but there are many other cases in which government leaders use this as an excuse to set up dictatorships. Sometimes the "excuse" results in real opposition to the government when basic human rights and freedoms are denied. But until the opposition succeeds in overthrowing the dictatorship, the lives of citizens are ruled by an iron fist.

When nations continue to ignore and abuse human rights of their citizens, they often plant the seeds of rebellion. People know when they are deprived of their basic rights. In the poor nation of Somalia a prisoner of conscience explained it this way to a reporter:

> Yes, I live in a nation that is poor. Yes, I live in a nation of hungry people. That I know because I have suffered great hunger myself, and I have cried as I watched two of my children die of starvation. And yes, my nation has seen terrible warfare. But how, I ask in God's name, does that give my government the right to torture me for my words and beliefs? As far as I am concerned, it doesn't.

Protecting the human rights of people is much more difficult than either defining them or drawing up declarations, bills

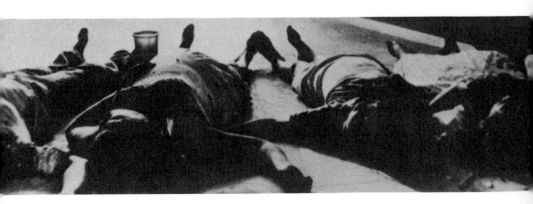

These people were killed by "death squads" in El Salvador.

44

of rights, and covenants. The major problem is that neither the United Nations or any other agency in the world has the power to force nations to honor all the rights of their citizens. Thus, it seems that until there is some agency that has such power or until the world becomes a more perfect place, the violations and abuses of human rights will continue to be a fact of life.

But that does not mean that such violations cannot be slowed down or, in some cases, prevented. In order for that to happen, people across the globe will have to speak up against such abuse. Eventually the acts of concerned nations and citizens may bring about a time when the dignity and rights of all peoples will be respected.

"If we were to select the most intelligent, imaginative, energetic, and emotionally stable third of mankind, all races would be represented."
—Franz Boas, anthropologist

3

Discrimination and Racism

On Sunday morning, September 15, 1963, at the black Sixteenth Street Baptist Church in Birmingham, Alabama, children were finishing their Sunday-school lesson, and services were about to begin. Suddenly, a bomb exploded. Windows blew out, parts of the walls and ceiling were ripped away, chairs and tables went flying in every direction. When the sound of the explosion passed, the crying and screaming of young children could be heard. "No, God! Oh, Lord! Please . . . No," pleaded one parent as people rushed to the aid of those who had been in the way of the blast. As parents and friends cleared away broken pieces of wood and plaster they found the bodies of four young black girls who had been killed. At least fifteen others were wounded. Robert Chambliss, a former member of a hate group called the Ku Klux Klan, was arrested for the murder of these children.

The Ku Klux Klan is one of a number of hate groups found in the United States. People who belong to these groups have a fear and hatred of people who are of a different race, religion, or nationality. At the center of their beliefs is the notion that some races are superior to others. The belief in a superior race and the acting out of hatred because of such beliefs is called racism.

Scientists have said time and again that race is merely a way of grouping people based upon physical characteristics and that race has nothing to do with how smart or how good or how bad people are. Race is just one way that scientists study different groups of people. The famous American anthropologist Franz Boas pointed out that "If we were to select the most intelligent, imaginative, energetic, and emotionally stable third of mankind, all races would be represented."

A cross is prominently displayed at a Ku Klux Klan meeting.

Nevertheless, many people believe that race somehow determines how people act and whether they are good or bad. Some of these people want to keep members of other races away. They believe that if people of different races "mix" or marry and have children with members of their own race, their race will no longer be pure or perfect. As one young woman racist explained, "People are like horses. If you mix a strong horse with a weak one, then the offspring will be weaker than the better one. So it is with people, the good race will become weaker." Of course, people are not like horses, and in a scientific sense, there is no such thing as a pure race. Nevertheless, the racist does not believe this. Racists often talk about the need to keep their race pure, and some will use violence to fight for this false belief.

The Reverend Richard G. Butler is the leader of an organization known as the Aryan Nations or Church of Jesus Christ Christian. According to Mr. Butler, ". . . there is no more sacred duty . . . no higher law to obey, than the battle for the existence of our Racial Nation. . . ." The Aryan Nations is a white racist group in the United States. They view black people as a "plague," a horrible disease which can spread. They also regard Jews as a race although there is no such thing as a Jewish race. For the racists, Jews are considered a race of "parasites," those who live off others.

Many of these racist groups call for the use of violence in the name of Christianity and to keep their race "pure." They twist Christian ideals of peace and the brotherhood of mankind into violence and hatred. In America, white racist groups include the Ku Klux Klan, Aryan Nations, National States' Rights party, Sheriff's Posse Comitatus, American Nazi party, and the CSA (The Covenant, The Sword, and the Arm of the Lord).

When racist beliefs and other forms of prejudice are acted

out, they deny people their human rights, including the right to live as in the case of the murder of the four schoolchildren in Birmingham. More recently, in June 1984, a Denver radio talk-show host, Alan Berg, was machine-gunned down as he arrived home. His killers are believed to have been members of the Aryan Nations. Berg, a Jew, had spoken out against white racist organizations. Today, white racist groups in America tend to focus most of their attacks on blacks and Jews.

Members of racist groups do not only commit crimes against people. In recent years, they have been involved in

This beach in South Africa is divided into one section for blacks and one section for whites.

armored car robberies in the states of California and Washington. It is believed that these acts are carried out to get money for their groups. Among other uses, the money is used for purchasing weapons and publishing hate literature. They point to crimes of murder and robbery committed by individuals of different races and religions as wrong and a threat to society. However, they see their own acts as patriotic and for the good of society. This twisted thinking permits them to carry out acts of violence in the name of their race and religion.

Those who deny human rights to others often justify their actions based upon beliefs and feelings about their victims. But, we might ask ourselves, how does one develop such beliefs or feelings that have caused so many innocent people to suffer? In order to answer this question, we might examine seven key words that help explain people's inhumanity toward others. These key words include prejudice, stereotyping, xenophobia, ethnocentrism, discrimination, scapegoating, and racism. They describe what people have learned as members of particular cultures and how they act toward others.

People and Culture

The planet earth is shared by more than five billion men, women, and children. They all share the same basic needs. Some of these needs are physical. Physical needs include food, shelter, and clothing. People also have psychological needs. Being accepted and loved by others and feeling good about one's own self are examples of psychological needs. While it may be possible to live alone as a hermit and still have physical needs met, many psychological needs require living in a group.

As people come to live together in groups, they form a way of life called culture. A group's culture includes language, religion, laws, customs, traditions, art, and music—anything that people learn as members of their group. So far, all of this may seem quite natural and harmless. After all, everyone belongs to at least one cultural group. However, a part of learning one's own culture often involves how to view those who are similar and those who are different. This can lead to either favorable or unfavorable feelings and beliefs about other groups.

Prejudice

Most cultures develop beliefs that help their members to notice the difference between their own kind and those of other cultures. These beliefs are learned in childhood and continue throughout one's life. The Hopi indians live in the southwestern part of the United States. When a Hopi child misbehaves, he or she may be told, "That is not the Hopi way." This is a way of saying, "Act the Hopi way and not like those who are different." It is common for children in almost every culture to be taught that members of other groups are different from them. By itself, this learning does not harm people. However, once differences are taught, they may lead people to believe that others are different and "ok" or different and "not as good." When children are taught that being different means another person or some group is evil or not as good as one's own group, then certain beliefs and feelings are formed. Other groups and their members may be viewed as strange, evil, or inferior.

Feelings and beliefs that are learned are called attitudes. We have attitudes about almost everything we know. Attitudes may be favorable or positive. Some attitudes may be unfavorable. When an attitude is unfavorable or negative, it may be due to prejudice.

Like all attitudes, prejudice is learned. Prejudice is a negative feeling or belief toward a group or person because he

52

or she is a member of that group. In addition, the prejudiced belief is fixed or rigid and not true about all members of the group.

You probably have heard or learned some things about other groups that are not true about all of their members. The following are false beliefs because they are not true about all members of the group:

"All black people are lazy."

"All Italians are gangsters."

"Polish people are stupid."

"All Jews are cheap."

"All white people are racists."

"Poor people don't want to work"

"Japanese are sly."

"Hispanics are thieves."

"All communists are evil."

When such beliefs are held or when unfavorable feelings develop from such beliefs, then we have a prejudiced attitude. These prejudices stand in the way of people getting along with each other. They are often passed on from one generation to another. For example, Julie may be encouraged by her parents and friends not to go out with Julio because he is Puerto Rican. The argument given against this relationship may be based upon the false beliefs that Puerto Ricans are violent, dirty, and loud. Julio's family and friends may point out that whites have no respect for tradition, no sense of family ties, and that Julio would be better off with a "good girl, a Puerto Rican girl." Such prejudiced beliefs are closely related to mental pictures that people hold of other groups. These pictures are called stereotypes.

Stereotyping

"It is almost noon," said the teacher, "so let us review our lesson. Karl, what have we learned?"

Karl replied, "How to recognize a Jew."

"Good, Tell us about it."

Karl answered, "The Jew can be recognized by his nose. It is crooked at the end and looks like the figure 6. The Jew nose is bent at the end."

"Is this the only way to tell a Jew?" asked the teacher.

"No. The Jew also is recognized by his thick lips and the lower lip hangs down—that is called the sloppy lip. The look of the Jew is lurking and sharp."

Lessons like the one above were taught in German schools during the Nazi period of the 1930s. Today, similar descriptions are mentioned in the hate literature of racist groups in the United States and elsewhere. This is true even though Jews come in all sizes and shapes with an equal variety of noses and looks. Jews are found in all three of the main racial stocks: Caucasian (white), Negroid (black), and Mongoloid (oriental). But the goal of such lessons was not to teach reality. Rather, the purpose was to instill a very rigid and false picture of a particular group in the minds of children. The lesson that Karl learned was designed to develop a stereotype.

As applied to people, the word stereotype was first used by American journalist Walter Lippmann. Mr. Lippman described a stereotype as a picture in the head. A stereotype differs from other mental pictures because it is fixed. This means that it does not change, and it is applied to all members of a group. Therefore, if you have a fixed mental picture of what Russians are like, and if you apply this mental picture to all Russians, then you have a stereotype.

For instance, if one has a stereotype that Russians are warlike, then he or she will regard each individual Russian as warlike regardless of what that person is really like. You can see how stereotyping helps create the fixed or rigid belief of a

In Madison Co. Court!
LARGE SALE OF
LAND AND NEGROES

Petition for Sale of Land and Slaves.

Albert G. McClellan and others

vs.

Mary Vaden and husband, G. W. Vaden and others, distributees of Isabella McClellan, dec'd.

In the above cause, the undersigned, Clerk of the County Court of Madison county, Tenn., as commissioner, will expose to public sale on Saturday, 24th of March next, at the Court house, in the town of Jackson, that most desirable and conveniently situated Tract of Land, known as the McClellan farm, containing

1000 ACRES.

in one body, and lying within a mile and a half of the town of Jackson. Also, at the same time and place,

18 Or 20 NEGROES,

consisting of men, women and children. The land will be divided into tracts previous to the day of sale, and each division will be sold seperately.

Terms of sale.—Land on a credit of one and two years, and the negroes upon a credit of 12 months from the day of sale. Notes, with good security, will be required of purchasers, and lien retained on both land and negroes for the purchase money. Title t the land and negroes indisputable.

P. C. McCOWAT,

C. & M. Commissioner.

Feb. 24, 1860.

A bill of sale for slaves dated February 24, 1860, is shown.

prejudiced attitude. You might try an experiment by asking some of your friends to describe what various groups are like. Some will probably present their stereotypes of the groups.

Xenophobia

The second special term is xenophobia, pronounced "zen-a-ʹfō-bē-a." Xenophobia means a fear of strangers. Quite often when people are faced with the unknown, they develop a fear. When we have a fear of people because we really do not understand them or because they are strangers, then we have what is called xenophobia. Fear leads people to imagine all sorts of unfavorable things about others. Fear can cause people to distort reality. This can lead to false beliefs and unfavorable feelings toward people who are physically different, follow different religions, or speak a different language.

Xenophobia can be found in the statements and beliefs of leaders and members of racist groups. Kerry Noble, one of the leaders of the racist group The Covenant, The Sword, and The Arm of the Lord (The CSA), remarked that "We do believe non-whites and Jews are a threat to our Christian, white race . . . Jews are training blacks to take over most of our cities." Of course, this is not true. Indeed, American blacks and Jews have enough trouble attempting to set aside prejudices that they hold toward each other. Xenophobia helps create prejudiced attitudes and acts of violence.

In the 1830s, Mormons settled in Missouri. Although they were Christians, they dressed differently and had different customs. For example, Mormon men were permitted to have more than one wife. They were also very successful in their work and stayed to themselves. To their non-Mormon neighbors, they seemed strange. Fear of Mormons and their way of life and success led to an order by Missouri governor Lillburn

W. Boggs. He ordered that all Mormons "must be treated as enemies and must be exterminated or driven from the state ... for the public good." The Mormons fled to Illinois, but some were killed, including women and children.

During World War II, Japanese Americans living on the West Coast of the United States were the object of fear and distrust. Japanese Americans belonged to the same racial group as those Japanese with whom America was at war. In addition, most whites had had little contact with Japanese Americans because they lived in segregated or racially separated areas. This and the fact that they were racially different made it easier for fear to spread among the white population. Rumors were spread that Japanese farmers were planting tomato fields in rows pointing toward American army and air bases. These rows were supposedly designed to aid Japanese pilots to their targets in the United States. This and other false rumors spread throughout the country.

The fear and distrust of anyone who looked "Jap" led the government to force Japanese Americans to live in concentration camps called relocation centers. Many lost their homes and livelihood. During this same period, Japanese American military units served for the United States in Italy. These units, the 100th and 442nd combat battalions, lost more than six hundred men and almost ten thousand were wounded. The 442nd battalion became the most decorated combat unit in the history of the American army. "While we were fighting and giving our lives for America, over one hundred thousand Japanese Americans were put in relocation camps. How odd it all seems" reflected a veteran from the 442nd battalion.

Xenophobia shows up in many ways. When Adie Williams, a black American soldier, arrived in Germany near the end of World War II, he was assigned to escort some prisoners to a rounding-up area.

"There was this one fella who was wet and shivering. I offered him a cigarette and lit it for him. He touched my hand as he took the cigarette. He got real scared and looked at his hand. He was surprised that my blackness didn't rub off."

Recently, xenophobia has also been a part of the cause of violence against Vietnamese and Cambodian immigrants to the United States. As new arrivals, many find it difficult to speak English, and their customs are unfamiliar to their neighbors. "When they first arrived, you could find them hunting for squirrels in the park . . . and they eat dogs!" commented a resident of northern California. Although squirrel hunting is an age-long tradition in America, it seems strange to city people to see others searching for squirrels in the city park. In America, a dog is regarded as a pet, "man's best friend," but to some Asians, a dog is food.

By keeping strong family ties and working as a unit, they are viewed as strange and a threat to others. Most of all, they are physically different in appearance and speak a different language. Jealousy over their ability to succeed in their work has led to name-calling and acts of violence against them and their property. Along the coast of Texas, fishing boats belonging to Vietnamese have been burned. In Denver, they experienced attacks against their property. Windows were smashed and some Vietnamese were threatened.

Along with xenophobia and stereotyping, there is another element to prejudiced attitudes. This is the belief and feeling of superiority. The notion that "we are better than they." It is called ethnocentrism.

Ethnocentrism

Ethnocentrism is the belief that one's group is superior to other groups. Ethnocentric beliefs include a love and blind loyalty for one's own culture or group and hatred for other groups. One might say that ethnocentric attitudes are strong prejudiced attitudes. Sometimes ethnocentric attitudes lead people to accuse others of disloyalty to their group. During the Vietnam War, many Americans opposed any criticism of American involvement in the war. Many other Americans saw the war as wrong and demonstrated against American participation in the war. The slogan "America! Love it or Leave it!" expressed the ethnocentric attitude that any criticism of the government's action was wrong and disloyal.

Ethnocentrism has shown up in the way teachers are supposed to teach children. In Florida, it once was required that teachers instruct students on the good qualities of "Americanism" and evils of communism. This state regulation reflected the notion that "we are good and opposition to our way is evil." As one teacher declared, "I do not oppose teaching children about other beliefs. So long as they first learn that our way is the true way." This may seem odd when we consider the large number of different groups and beliefs in America. The state regulation has been changed largely due to the efforts of teachers who believe that children should be allowed to learn about different systems and beliefs of other countries without being brainwashed by learning only the evils of one system and the good points of another.

Ethnocentric attitudes and beliefs are found throughout the world. In Iran, the government of Ayatollah Ruhollah Khomeini emphasizes that Iran is the nation of God while the United States is viewed as the devil, and the American way of life is viewed as evil. For many Russians, the United States is regarded as a nation bent on war and conquest. At the same time, these people view themselves as peace loving and belonging to the best "state in the world."

Stereotyping, xenophobia, and ethnocentrism combine to help create and reinforce prejudices. But, as the world famous social scientist, Gordon Allport, pointed out, prejudice if kept to one's own self will not do any great social harm. The problem, Dr. Allport continued, was that prejudice is seldom kept to oneself.

Discrimination

When Dr. John Greene and his wife Mildred inquired about purchasing a house on Carte Drive in Tampa, Florida, they were told the house was just sold. "We are very sorry, but we just signed the contract and have not had time to take down the for sale sign." explained the owner. John and Mildred left. At about the same time, another couple approached the house. The owner said, "Yes, yes, the house is open for inspection. Please come in." The Greenes were walking to their car when they overheard these comments.

The facts that Dr. Greene was a professor and Ms. Greene was a schoolteacher were of no importance. Nor was it important that the Greenes were willing and able to pay the asking price for the house. The owner only knew that they were black. The treatment the Greenes received was the acting out of prejudice. This is called discrimination.

Discrimination is the unequal treatment of one group toward another. The group that discriminates is usually in power. Its members tend to control the government. They can pass laws favorable to themselves and unfavorable to the victims of discrimination.

For many years in the United States, some states such as Virginia, Mississippi, Texas, Arkansas, and Alabama required people to pay a poll tax in order to vote. Requiring one to own property and passing a reading or literacy test were other ways of limiting who could or could not vote. The effect of these laws was to limit the number of voters who were black or poor. In 1964, the Twenty-fourth Amendment to the Constitution of the United States was ratified. It outlawed the use of the poll tax as a requirement in federal elections. Other laws and court decisions limited the use of literacy tests in order to prevent discrimination against racial minorities.

In South Africa, the government is controlled by whites. The white-controlled government has created laws that keep blacks and Coloureds (people of black and white or black and Asian ancestry) from having equal rights. Blacks and Coloureds are not allowed to take part in running the government. They do not have the right to have a part in the making of laws, and if they object to unfair laws, they may be put in prison, beaten, or killed.

An example of the poor living conditions black people are forced to live under in Soweto, South Africa, is shown here.

Because they have the political power, the group that discriminates may also control all or much of the economic system in its society. It may see to it that good-paying jobs and ownership of good land remain in the group's hands. Others who are not members of their group receive low-paying jobs and may be denied the right to own land or property unless the group with power permits it. Political power also leads to social power. This means that those holding political power can determine where people may live, if they will receive an education, be permitted to be served in hospitals, restaurants, or use public transportation. In fact, the group that discriminates may actually determine who is a member of which group.

Those who have the power and discriminate are called the social majority or simply the majority. Those who are discriminated against are called the social minority or minority. The size of the group does not determine who is called the majority or minority. It is a question of who has the power. This may seem a little confusing for us since we are so used to using majority in the political sense where it means more than half of the total number in a group. Nevertheless, when you hear people refer to minorities as those people who are discriminated against, you will know that it is not the size of the group that counts. It is whether or not they are given equal treatment in society.

For example, in South Africa, the whites are the social majority, but they only make up 16 percent of the total population. The blacks and Coloureds are the minority although they comprise over 81 percent of the population. Here, size of the group does not determine who is called the majority or minority. Again, it is a matter of who has the political, economic, and social power in the society. Discrimination can be economic, social, or political. However, discrimination is only one way that prejudices can be acted out. Another way is called scapegoating.

Scapegoating
Scapegoating is an expression of hostility, anger, or violence against a group or its members based upon prejudiced attitudes. The person who scapegoats blames an entire group for some wrong of which it may be partially or totally innocent. Scapegoating may range from name-calling to violence and murder.

There are different motives for scapegoating. Dr. Allport suggested that one might seek a scapegoat for political means. Such a person seeks to become a popular leader by attacking a group and blaming it for all of society's problems. He or she tries to convince people that if they follow him or her then together they will wipe out the evil ones. Hitler was an example of such a person. He blamed communists and Jews for the

This is a copy of the passbook all black people in South Africa were forced to carry (until very recently) at all times.

defeat of Germany in World War I and for the problems facing Germany after that war.

Some people act this way because they want to be accepted by others. They go along with the crowd. They often attended lynchings or hangings of blacks in the South and even participated in the burning, hanging, and mutilating of lynch victims.

Others find scapegoating a convenient way to blame their own fears, weaknesses, or mistakes on others. In Uganda, during the rule of Idi Amin, Asians were made the object of scapegoating. They had prospered in Uganda, and this caused jealousy among black Ugandans. Under Amin's rule and with the support of many black Africans, Asians were falsely blamed for ruining the economy of the country and of being disloyal to Uganda.

Based upon these false charges, Asians were forced to live in the countryside near the desert of Karamoja—a place where few people would want to live, and where life would be difficult. Finally, Amin forced the Asians to leave Uganda. He claimed that the need to remove the Asians came to him in a dream. Many Ugandans believed that removing Asians would improve their economic way of life. But their goal of improving their economy by depriving others of their human rights ended in failure.

Racism
Racism is a combination of prejudiced attitudes and acts of discrimination and scapegoating against a particular group or number of groups. Racism differs from other forms of prejudice in that it emphasizes the false notion that racial differences among people are a cause of social differences. The racist believes that race determines how people will behave and if people are good or bad.

The racist also believes that his or her race is superior to all other racial groups, and therefore, his or her group must protect itself against "mixing" with others. By mixing, they mean interracial marriages or marriages between people of different groups. A racist may identify a group as a different race although in a scientific sense, the group is not a race. Although Jews are found among all racial stocks, Jewish people have been falsely referred to as a race.

Racists often do things that are in contradiction to what they say or believe is true. Earlier, it was shown that German children were taught how to recognize a Jew, but the German government made the Jewish people wear the Jewish Star of David with the word "Jude" printed on it in order to be recognized. While the term Aryan actually refers to a language system, Hitler used it to describe himself and his superrace, which would conquer the world. The ideal Aryans were described by Hitler and his followers as tall, blond-haired, blue-eyed Europeans. But Hitler was himself a rather short man with dark hair. When Japan and Germany became allies during World War II, Japanese who were certainly not even close to being "Aryan" were declared honorary Aryans by Hitler.

These inconsistent actions are not limited to the past. In South Africa, some important black visitors are declared to be white in order that they may receive services only permitted to whites. There is also a report from South Africa that a young girl whose parents were white seemed to have what officials decided were black features, such as having somewhat darker skin. Therefore, she was reclassified by the South African government as a Coloured. She lost all of the rights that she previously enjoyed as a "white person."

These examples of how the idea of race is misused by people has led some scientists to suggest that the entire notion of race be dropped. It is obvious that race is often used as a tool by those who wish to build up their own group and put or keep members of other groups down.

Even Adolf Hitler admitted that race was a meaningless idea. Privately, he admitted to a friend, "I know perfectly well . . . that in a scientific sense there is no such thing as a race. But . . . with the conception of race, National Socialism will . . . recast the world."

A simple way of noticing racist beliefs and behaviors is to look for buildups and put-downs. Buildups are those beliefs and actions that attempt to show how one group is superior to other groups. Put-downs are those attempts to show or treat other groups as inferior. In both cases, the reasons for the buildups or put-downs must be related to the idea of race. Hitler built up the German people by suggesting that they were a superior race. He put down Gypsies, Jews, and others as inferior. Early European explorers and settlers viewed themselves as civilized and those whom they met in foreign lands as savages or "pagans," terms that are put-downs.

Prejudice, discrimination, and racism have blossomed and thrived in many places throughout the world. They have destroyed many lives and deprived millions of people of their human rights. Even in the United States whose Declaration of Independence states that all people are created equal and endowed with the right to life, liberty, and the pursuit of happiness, discrimination and racism have been destructive social diseases.

Discrimination and Racism in the United States
At first, one may not think that discrimination is as harmful as scapegoating. But discrimination can be terrifying. It can deprive people of the ability to provide for their basic needs. There is a saying that "man does not live by bread alone." This means that there are important things other than just

one's work or employment that provide for the basic needs of people. Nevertheless, without "bread" neither man nor woman can live at all. When you are denied a job because of the color of your skin, your religion, nationality, or other cultural trait, or even your sex or age, then you are a victim of economic discrimination.

In the United States, the list of groups of people who have suffered from economic discrimination is extremely long. It includes Irish, Germans, Italians, Puerto Ricans, Mexicans, Cubans, Chinese, Poles, Japanese, Native Americans, Jews, Catholics, blacks, women, and the elderly. Of all of these groups, black Americans and Native Americans have suffered most from racism in America.

Black Americans. Because people hold prejudices that are based on negative stereotypes, they tend to deny others certain types of jobs. Blacks have been stereotyped as unintelligent and lazy. Therefore, many black Americans have been denied employment that pays well. On the other hand, it has been a common stereotype that blacks are good at low-paying jobs such as housecleaning, baby-sitting, washing dishes, and sweeping floors in restaurants. Racial discrimination has caused many able and educated blacks to take low-paying jobs. Prejudice and discrimination have deprived many blacks from advancing and have deprived America of some potentially great contributors to society. The seed of prejudice and its blossom, discrimination, has deprived all America.

For years, black children were denied equal education with whites. American society was largely two societies—one black, the other white. This is what is meant by a segregated society. It is a society where people are physically separated because of their race, religion, or some other characteristic. In 1954, the Supreme Court ruled that black children could not be forced to attend segregated or racially separate schools. When Congress passed the Civil Rights Act of 1964, the walls of segregation began to tumble.

The Civil Rights Act of 1964 prohibited discrimination. Blacks and other racial and cultural minorities could not be legally discriminated against when attempting to vote, find a job, or seek service at a restaurant. More and more blacks were to benefit from education. Job opportunities for minorities increased. In 1968, the United States government passed the Fair Housing Act which prohibited real-estate companies from discriminating against minorities when selling houses. Nevertheless, the scars of slavery followed by segregation could not be overcome immediately and neither could prejudiced attitudes.

Today, most communities in America remain segregated, and approximately one-third of all blacks live in poverty. Poor housing and unemployment breed crime and other social ills. Major problems facing blacks in inner cities of the United States include crimes committed by blacks against blacks, teenage pregnancy, the breakup of families, drug abuse, and high unemployment which is almost 50 percent among black teenagers. Even in courts of justice, many believe that blacks are more likely to receive harsher punishments than whites for the same offense. This is especially true if the victims of a crime are white.

In addition to discrimination, blacks and other minorities have been the victims of racist' acts. More than five thousand blacks have been lynched in the United States since the end of the American Civil War in 1865; many others have been beaten or abused for no other reason than they were black. What happened to Michael Griffith illustrates how racial violence can spring up at any moment.

The Saturday night sky of December 20, 1986, was partly

cloudy. The temperature hovered at a mild 46° F (8° C). Michael Griffith, his stepfather, and a friend were driving through the Howard Beach neighborhood of New York City. The car developed engine trouble. The three men began walking in search of a phone. After walking about three miles, they came to a pizza parlor. Told there was no phone they could use, they ordered a pizza. Having completed their snack, the three left the parlor.

Suddenly, they were surround by a group of white men. "Niggers don't belong here!" one shouted. Then the whites attacked the three blacks. Griffith and his two friends ran, but they were caught and beaten again. Eventually, Griffith reached a highway. While being chased, he attempted to escape by crossing the road. Griffith was struck and killed by a passing motorist. Those responsible for beating and chasing Griffith were arrested and charged with the attack. Three days later, in another area of New York, a group of black youths sought revenge by attempting to attack a white teenager waiting for a bus. He was rescued by other whites in the area.

Racism had taken another life and planted seeds of hatred in others. New York mayor, Edward Koch, summarized these incidents by remarking that "Anyone who says the country is free . . . of racism . . . is not telling the truth or is simply an ostrich whose head is in the sand."

One month later the United States celebrated the birthday of Martin Luther King, Jr. Before being felled by an assassin's bullet in 1968, Dr. King had dedicated his life to helping combat racism in America. He is regarded as one of the great civil rights leaders in American history. Dr. King was the first black American whose birthday was declared a national holiday. When a parade was held to honor Dr. King's memory in Cumming, Georgia, members of the Ku Klux Klan and

Martin Luther King, Jr., was a major leader of the U.S. Civil Rights Movement.

American Nazi party demonstrated against the marchers. "Go home, niggers!" and "We hate niggers!" accompanied threats of violence and stone throwing. Within one month after the march, the local Ku Klux Klan of Cumming reported that its membership had increased by three hundred new members!

White Hate, Black Hate. As a reaction to white racism, black racist groups have emerged from time to time in America. The Nation of Islam or Black Muslims, founded in the 1930s by Elijah Muhammad, encouraged the beliefs that whites were a cursed race, "white devils," inferior and evil. Like some white racist groups, they formed their own military-like group. The group was known as the Fruit of Islam. After Elijah Muhammad's death in 1975, his son Imam Warith Deen Muhammad moved the religious body in a more tolerant direction. The name had been changed to the American Muslim Mission. By 1985, nonblacks were permitted to join.

The Ku Klux Klan march in Washington, D.C., in 1928.

In 1978, Louis Farrakhan, who had been a follower of Elijah Muhammad since 1955 and an officer in the movement, broke with the main body of Black Muslims and formed his own group under the original name of the Nation of Islam. The Fruit of Islam became his bodyguards. Farrakhan appears to hate whites and especially Jews. In 1984, Farrakhan referred to Hitler as a great man and called the creation of the Jewish state of Israel an "outlaw act."

Native Americans. The story of the Native American differs from that of blacks and other minority groups in America. From almost the first contact between Native Americans and Europeans, a struggle developed between them. Europeans sought to take Native American lands and in some cases to convert Native Americans to Christianity. Racist beliefs were used along with force to justify these goals. The Native American was considered a savage who needed to be removed or civilized. Therefore, it was thought only right that whites should take what they needed.

After the United States was formed, whites continued to move onto Native American lands. Eventually, Native Americans were forced to live on reservations. Reservations were lands given to the Native Americans for settlement. These lands were thought to be unusable by white peoples. In time, if it were found that the land was usable, it was taken away and other, more barren land was given to the Native Americans.

The story of the treatment of Native Americans was one of conquest, murder, and removal. The racist attitudes toward Native Americans led to the notion that Native Americans could only be civilized if their way of life was destroyed and if they learned the ways of the white American. In 1824 the Bureau of Indian Affairs was created by the U.S. government. The Bureau of Indian Affairs was headed by a commissioner. It was the commissioner's job to manage the relationships of Native Americans and the U.S. government and between Native Americans and other non–Native Americans such as settlers.

In 1872, Francis A. Walker, the commissioner of Indian affairs, stated that Native American tribes must be "reduced to the condition of suppliants [one who asks humbly for charity] . . . If they stand up against the progress of civilization . . . they must be crushed. . . . They must yield or perish." Walker viewed the Native Americans as uncivilized. The road to civilization was to beat them into the ground and then change them into more humanlike beings.

The bureau set up schools on the reservations. In these BIA (Bureau of Indian Affairs) schools, Native American children were taught English and the white American way of life.

In 1882, Indian Affairs Commissioner Hiram Price wrote the following statement regarding the role of education for Native American children: ". . . thousands of Indian children now roaming wild shall be taught to speak the English language and earn their own living, [the government schools will change] . . . the wild, roaming Indian into an industrious, peaceable, law-abiding citizen." The goal of the Bureau of Indian Affairs was to destroy the Native American culture by replacing it with the culture of white America.

Today, there are still BIA schools. These schools still attempt to have Native American children move away from their culture and become more like the white Americans. However, some reservations have schools run by Native Americans. Here, Native American language and traditions are respected and taught along with other subjects.

The life of the Native American has been made difficult by discrimination and prejudiced attitudes. Oftentimes, racism and prejudices of the past are handed down from one generation to the next. The attitudes of such people as Walker and Price were shared and passed on by many Americans. As late as 1967, even schoolbooks expressed one-hundred-year-old racist attitudes toward Native American groups. One social studies textbook, *Missouri: Midland State,* gave the following false description of the Osage Indians: "They were said to be greasy and disgusting objects with dirty buffalo robes thrown over their shoulders. The women, if possible, were more filthy and disgusting than the men."

A band of Apache Indian prisoners sit at a rest stop beside the Southern Pacific Railway, near Nueces River, Texas, 1886. Among those on their way to forced exile in Florida are Natchez (*center front*) and, *to the right,* Geronimo and his son in matching shirts.

Many of today's Native American children are caught between two worlds. There are the Native American cultures with their rich traditions, language, and history. Among some Native Americans, their way of life expects people to live in tune with nature and all living things. Yet, Native American children often are taught to disregard this way of life and become part of another world, "the white man's world," which has different values and beliefs. This is a world that has other advantages. Some Native American children cannot adjust to these conflicting ways. They become confused and do not know who or what they really are. They lose their sense of group identity. This may help explain why Native American teenagers have one of the highest suicide rates in the United States. Senator Edward M. Kennedy described the treatment of Native Americans as "a national tragedy and a national disgrace."

Women: The Largest Social Minority. One might expect that in a democracy like the United States, men and women would have the same basic human rights. However, although women make up more than 50 percent of the population, they have been victims of discrimination and abuse in both the public sector and in their private lives.

Traditionally, women in American economic life have been limited in their opportunities to enter many of the same occupations and professions as men. They were expected to be housewives, teachers, secretaries, or nurses. Today, more and more women have entered occupations formerly closed to them. But discrimination, unfair employment practices, and sexual harassment still exist.

A woman with the same work experience as a man is often paid less for the same job. In addition, women are more likely to be promoted at a slower rate than men, and few attain top executive positions in major companies. In some cases, they are expected to provide services which are demeaning. For example, a woman working in the same office and at the same job as a man may be asked to do favors such as buying coffee for others or answering the phone while the man continues doing what he was hired to do.

Many women are not considered good employment risks simply because of a variety of prejudices and false stereotypes—such as the idea that a woman is too emotional, or that she will miss work every time her child is ill. With a growing number of single parents, most of whom are women, the need for equal job opportunities and recognition is essential to women and to the economic life of the nation.

Aside from discrimination in the employment field, women have suffered from political discrimination as well. In his book *Birth of the Constitution,* Edmund Lindop briefly describes the long struggle women carried on in the United States to gain the right to vote. This goal was pursued from 1848 until the ratification of the Nineteenth Amendment to the Constitution in 1920.

While other nations such as England, India, Israel, and more recently, the Philippines have elected a woman to high office, the United States has never had a woman president. Nevertheless, women have made and continue to make progress in the political life of the nation. In 1916 Jeannette Rankin became the first woman elected to the House of Representatives. Many women have since played significant roles in the federal government. The first woman associate justice of the United States Supreme Court, Sandra Day O'Connor, was appointed in 1981. On a state level, the first woman governor was elected in 1924, and more women are being elected as mayors and council members than ever before.

Yet against all this progress, women are still the victims of various forms of discrimination in their private lives. While many women enjoy equal partnership in marriages and in other family relationships, many others are not so fortunate. They suffer mental and physical abuses that may range from name-calling and threats to beatings and outright murder. According to one estimate, almost two million American women are victims of wife-beating each year. From April 1985 until the end of that year, New York City police arrested 1000 men for wife-beating and another unmarried 779 men for beating the women with whom they were living.

The effects of being beaten are not merely physical. They create emotional wounds as well. In 1985, the private psychiatric Hartgrove Hospital in Chicago created a special medical unit to deal specifically with the problems of women, including those resulting from physical and mental abuse. This was the first such special unit established in the United States.

In addition, safe houses for abused women and their children have been set up throughout the land. In some ways they are similar to the first safe house for women established in England in 1974 by Erin Pizzey. In her book *Scream Quietly or the Neighbors Will Hear* she describes many of the experiences of abused women in England—the cruelty they suffered and in some cases their successes in overcoming these experiences.

Although the main focus has been on the United States, violations against the human rights of women extend to many if not most nations around the world. As early as 1954, this problem was recognized, and the United Nations issued the Convention on the Political Rights of Women , calling for the universal right of women to vote and hold public office. Yet, it was not until 1976 that the United States signed this convention. In 1979, the United Nations General Assembly adopted the   Convention on the Elimination of All Forms of Discrimination Against Women .   Both of these conventions may serve to guide nations toward eliminating human rights abuses against women.

The Dilemma Continues

In the 1940s, Swedish social scientist, Gunnar Myrdal, described the United States as a nation with a dilemma, a problem that has conflicting choices. On the one hand, he noted that Americans believe in equality, justice, and human dignity for all peoples. On the other hand, he found that these beliefs come into conflict with the way Americans treat each other because of racial or religious differences. To Myrdal, Americans seemed torn between democratic beliefs and undemocratic behavior. Today, the American dilemma, as he called it, is still alive.

Discrimination and racism did not find a home only in America. They have raised their ugly heads in many parts of the world. In virtually every nation on every continent some form of discrimination and racism can be found. Today, one of the most racist policies exists in the Republic of South Africa.

South Africa: Apartheid

In the Republic of South Africa, racism has denied black Africans basic human rights. The South African government has developed a policy called apartheid (pronounced "a-part-tīt"). The word apartheid means apartness or separation. This policy is made to keep the power of government and wealth of South Africa in the hands of the white population. South Africa's former prime minister Hendrik F. Verwoerd described the purpose of apartheid in his country as "nothing else than this: we want to keep South Africa white . . . Keeping it white can mean only one thing, namely, white domination—not leadership, not guidance but control, supremacy."

The apartheid policy of today is made up of laws that prevent black Africans from enjoying the same rights as whites. Apartheid grew out of the history of South Africa, and has some similarities with America's experience with racism.

The first white settlement in South Africa took place in 1652. During the early period, slavery was introduced. Since the local Africans resisted slave labor, white settlers imported black slaves from the north. Eventually, slavery was abolished.

However, unlike the American experience, white South Africans were few in number compared to black South Africans. By the time the Republic of South Africa was formed in 1910, the population was made up of four major groups. These were black Africans or Bantu-speaking people, Asians, whites, and people of mixed black and white ancestry. The latter are called Coloureds. Whites made up only about 16

Winnie Mandela, a South African human rights activist, salutes her supporters just before being "banned" by the South African government.

percent of the population. The blacks made up about 70 percent, Coloureds 11 percent, and Asians comprised the remainder. Being so outnumbered, the whites lived in constant fear of losing control over the black Africans. They also wanted to continue to take advantage of cheap black African labor.

To keep the black people down and to maintain control over the nation, the white government passed laws to prevent blacks from improving their lives. In 1948, the term apartheid came into common use. It described the policy of keeping nonwhites from sharing in the benefits of South African life.

Under the policy of apartheid, blacks can live only in certain areas. Although they make up over 70 percent of the population, they are only permitted to own or settle on 13 percent of the land. This leaves most of the land for whites who make up only 15 percent of the population. Black chil-

This beach in Durban, South Africa, is reserved for white people only.

dren and adults are not allowed to attend the same schools, movie theaters, restaurants, or parks as whites. Certain beaches, all passenger trains, and even buses are segregated or racially separated by signs that read Whites Only and Coloureds.

Hospitals for whites will not allow blacks to be treated, even in emergencies. Black medical services are very poor and supplies lacking. In one black hospital, some patients do not have beds. They must lie on the floor and use dirty sheets. Some bathrooms do not even have toilet paper. Medicine and equipment to treat the sick are often lacking. By contrast, white hospitals are well equipped and patients are well treated. As a result of such discrimination, it is no surprise that black children suffer from more diseases and die more often than white children. For many black Africans, apartheid is more than merely a question of freedom; it is a matter of life and death.

A security guard in Johannesburg, South Africa, arrests a black man for protesting apartheid.

In order to maintain control over blacks and Coloureds, the government until very recently required that they carry identification passbooks. These passbooks contained the holder's fingerprints, photograph, employment records, and permits to enter certain areas. To take advantage of cheap black labor, the government allowed blacks to work in restricted areas. Sometimes men are taken for almost a year at a time, and they are not given the opportunity to see their families during this time.

Banning is another way that is used to keep blacks down. Blacks can be banned if the government thinks they are troublemakers. A banned person is placed under house arrest. That means that he or she cannot leave his or her home from 6:00 P.M. until 6:00 A.M. during the week and all day and night on Sundays. A banned person cannot have visitors to his or her home or attend school or enter a factory. When a

A man shows a passbook in Cape Town, South Africa.

person is banned, he or she becomes a "nonperson," a prisoner in his or her own home.

Any black who challenges the white authority may be arrested. His or her her home may be destroyed. When a Zulu woman went to find her husband who had been arrested for being in a restricted area, her home was bulldozed by the government. Upon returning home, she protested and tried to remain at the place where her house once stood. Police dragged her away and arrested her. Friends took care of her children, but she was sentenced to three years in jail. If arrested, a black person might be tortured and might be kept in jail for years without a trial.

For many South African whites, apartheid is more than a racist policy. It is a basic value. To these people, their survival rests upon keeping blacks and Coloureds segregated and subjugated. They believe that without apartheid they and their nation will be destroyed. Yet, there are a number of whites who oppose apartheid. These opponents claim that if South Africa is to survive, then apartheid must be abolished. Many believe that apartheid is doomed and the only question is whether it will be abolished by law or by civil war. "The more resistance against apartheid, the more the government will resist. It is like a rope. Two sides are pulling. When it snaps, someone must fall," observed a white South African teenager whose family has given up and moved to another country.

Patterns of Discrimination and Racism in the Soviet Union.
In the Soviet Union, one finds various forms of discrimination. One particular form of discrimination is political discrimination. Even though the Soviet Union claims to guarantee freedom of speech, many Russian citizens bitterly joke that the "only difference between freedom of speech in

America and in Russia is that in America there is freedom AFTER speech." If a person's views are not in agreement with government policy, then such a person may be sent to special camps called *kolonii poseleniya* or settlement colonies. Here, one remains to carry out "corrective labor" until such time that he or she is considered fit to return to society. Being fit means to conform to the policies and beliefs of the government. Corrective labor is a form of slave labor. It may include road repairs, cutting down trees, working on loading docks or in mines. Living conditions are poor. Food is scarce. Clothing is insufficient. Many do not survive the more difficult camps.

Discrimination against religious groups is common in the Soviet Union. Russian Orthodox, Baptist, Lutheran, Evangelical, and other Christian groups are harassed. Leaders are imprisoned, and their followers are harassed. Official government discrimination has led to unofficial acts of violence among individuals.

According to one report out of the Soviet Union, twenty-year-old Ivan Moiseev had been drafted into the Soviet army. When his fellow comrades noticed that he was a devout Baptist, he was beaten and tortured. According to the report, Ivan survived the beatings. Then while the commanding officer Lieutenant Colonel Malsin looked on, Ivan was thrown into the Black Sea and drowned.

In the past, life in Russia for the Jews was like a "fiddler on the roof"—uncertain and at any moment likely to fall. At any moment, a Jewish village might be attacked, and its inhabitants slaughtered. Near the turn of the century, in Kishinev, Russia, a false rumor led to the murder of forty-seven Jews. Many were babies and young children who had nails driven into their heads and who were thrown out of second-story windows. The police delayed for two days before moving in to stop the attacks.

Although pogroms or organized violent attacks against Jews ended under Soviet rule, discrimination and scapegoating are still a problem. Jews are mocked, arrested, and periodically harassed. Many have attempted to leave the Soviet Union. Some have succeeded; others are denied permission to leave. Many are even afraid to ask for permission. Ludmilla and her family succeeded. Today, Ludmilla, called Lucy by her American friends, recounts some of the experiences she encountered as a Jew wanting to leave the Soviet Union.

By the time she was twenty, she was married and had her first child. While in the hospital she shared a maternity room with seven other women.

They called me little black girl, kike, and dirty Jew. I cried a lot. They said that it was too bad that Hitler did not kill all of the Jews and that Stalin should have finished the job. I knew then that I had to get out of Russia with my child.

In order to get permission to leave, I had to get myself expelled from the Komsomol or Communist Youth Movement. I had graduated from the Leningrad Conservatory of Music. So, I had to return and get expelled from the Komsomol. At the meeting of the Komsomol, the group leader humiliated me. She said, "How can you do such a thing? How can you leave the best Party in the world? You are a snake. You will be sorry and want to return to us. But we will spit on you. We shall use your blood to paint our houses." I had to remain very silent. I was called all sorts of names. The leader said, "You Jews are the cause of all of our problems."

I wanted to speak up, but a KGB, secret police, official was there. If I spoke back then he might arrest me. Send me to a slave labor camp or jail. Finally, the leader said that she hoped my baby would die and that he was a Jew snake like me. I could not take that so I spoke back. "You are blind with hate. You hate because you have such a low opinion of yourself." I screamed, "You will probably never have a baby. No man could want someone so hateful as you." The KGB officer pulled me by the arm and led me out of the room. The two hours of humiliation were over, but now I would be arrested. But I could not stand it when she cursed my baby. Outside the room, the KGB officer gently told me to leave and wished me good luck. I was shocked. I thought maybe it was a trick, but it wasn't. He really let me go.

The Soviet Union consists of many ethnic groups. School textbooks are printed in over fifty languages and the state-run radio sends out news in over sixty languages. Information regarding racial and ethnic violence in the Soviet Union is difficult to receive. Nevertheless, conflicts between Russians and other minorities have been reported. These conflicts with Russians have included Moslem Kazakhs in Central Asia and Yakuts in Siberia. The source for these conflicts appears to be an unwillingness on the part of minorities to give up their identity for a unified Russian culture.

Japan. Discrimination and racism also occur in other parts of the world. In Japan, Koreans are faced with discrimination in housing and employment. The source of this discrimination may be the result of years of conflict between the two cultures. Traditional Japanese society consisted of a caste system. A caste is a social class that is closed. People born into a caste are locked into it for life.

The only way to escape from one's caste would be to change occupation, name, and place of residence. Woodworkers, ironworkers, tanners, and butchers made up various low castes based upon occupation. With technological changes in Japan, these castes have virtually disappeared. One group, the Eta, who deal in fish are still present. Prejudiced attitudes toward the Eta are common, but since they are racially indistinguishable from other Japanese, there is less discrimination than in other cases. Eta are believed to be dirty and "untouchable."

The Ainu are a racially distinct group. They are outcasts in Japanese society and remain mainly in isolated areas. Their integration into Japanese society is hampered by cultural differences and prejudices. But their racially "white" characteristics are highly regarded by the Japanese. Traditional Japanese society puts a favorable premium on "white skin"— "A white woman's skin overcomes seven other defects in women" is an old Japanese proverb.

The most racist attitude found among Japanese is directed toward blacks. "How could we ever face your ancestors?" lamented a Japanese mother to her daughter who desired to marry a black American visitor.

Great Britain. Before 1900, England had been a predominantly white, Christian nation. With the exception of a Jewish minority, the British were isolated from other ethnic or racial groups. As the British Empire began to crumble, people from various colonies throughout the world moved to England. They came from India, Africa, the West Indies, and the Far East. As long as their numbers were small and they remained isolated or in low-level jobs, the friction between former colonial subjects and the whites of England was not a problem.

As their numbers increased and as they began to compete for decent standards of living and employment, racial prejudices, discrimination, and violence emerged. "They are rubbish, and they stink" and "They're lazy" are some of the comments made regarding racial minorities in the London area. A survey completed in 1985 found that one third of the employers surveyed discriminated against black people trying to find work.

In 1981, dwellings of black families were set on fire, black women, children, and men were killed. In 1985, racial violence spread throughout major cities of Great Britain including London, Liverpool, and Birmingham. A major concern regarding racial unrest has been the lack of police protection for minorities and racism among police officials. This racial violence has been linked to the poor relations between police and racial minorities.

A Global Problem

Great Britain is not alone among European countries faced with problems of racial prejudices, discrimination, and violence. France, Belgium, the Netherlands, Switzerland, and West Germany have experienced problems of racism in recent years.

Prejudice, discrimination, and racism are not limited to one nation or continent. They are worldwide. The Chinese are discriminated against in Indonesia, Malaysia, and the Philippines. In Iran, members of the Bahá'í religion are victims of state-sponsored discrimination and scapegoating. Jews remain the object of discrimination and racism in the Soviet Union, the United States, South Africa, Iraq, and most other nations throughout the world. Christian groups also have been targets of discrimination in Egypt and the Soviet Union at various times. In South America, racist attitudes are expressed against blacks in Brazil, and Indians have been exterminated in Paraguay.

The problem of discrimination and racism is not one that can be fought with guns or bombs. A cure for this social disease cannot be bought with money. Laws can and have been passed to prevent discrimination and racist acts. But discrimination and racism are linked to attitudes that live in the minds of people. Eventually, these attitudes are acted out—legally or illegally.

The battle against discrimination and racism might best be fought by the commitment and recognition of each individual that people are entitled to the same basic rights regardless of color, nationality, religion, or other cultural trait. Until that time, the seeds of prejudice will take root. Its blossoms, discrimination and racism, will bloom. Like all flowers, they will go to seed and be scattered by the winds of xenophobia, ethnocentrism, and stereotyping—to be planted in the minds of others.

4

Genocide

Slaughter. Bloodbaths. All-out or partial destruction. Mass executions. Exterminations. Mass political killings. Purges. Pogroms. These are some of the terms and phrases that are usually used to describe acts of genocide.

The term "genocide" was coined in 1944 by a lawyer named Raphael Lemkin. *Geno* means "a tribe or race" of people. *Cide* means "to cut or kill." Genocide has come to mean the *deliberate* destruction or murder of a *particular* group of people. It is usually committed because one group (often government officials) distrusts or despises a particular group because of its race, religion, ethnic background, political beliefs, or nationality.

In this context, the word "destruction" can mean a number of different things. It could mean the murder, in part or whole, of a particular group of people. Sometimes the killings number in the hundreds, thousands, or even millions. For instance, the Nazis slaughtered over six million Jewish people (as well as six million others) during the years 1936–1945.

"Destruction" could also mean deliberate actions, aside from outright murder, that bring about the end of a particular group. For example, it could mean the planned starvation of a group of people. This actually happened between 1932 and 1933 when the Soviet Union carried out a policy that led to the starvation of up to ten million Ukrainian people.

Or the term "destruction" could also mean the establishment of laws that try to prevent births within a group. Such an action could result in the eventual extinction or end of the entire group.

Genocide is vastly different from homicide. *Homo* is the biological name for "human." *Cide,* of course, means to "kill." Homicide, then, refers to the murder of one person or ten. But it does not refer to the destruction of the lives of hundreds, let alone thousands or millions, like genocide does.

Numerous experts point out that many, if not most, homicides are not planned. They often just happen on the spur of the moment. For instance, a person may get so furious during an argument that he or she ends up killing someone. Or, a person who is robbing a store may get into a gunfight and kill someone. Genocide, on the other hand, is usually carried out according to a specific plan.

War also should not be confused with acts of genocide, even though genocide can and sometimes does take place during wartime. War is usually defined as "an armed struggle between opposing forces in order to accomplish a particular goal." Genocide, however, is the planned murder of a group of people because they are "different" in some way or hated for some reason.

Also, in a war both sides usually do everything they can to win. Each side uses all of its soldiers and as many of its weapons as it needs to. But during acts of genocide it is a vastly different situation. Sometimes the victims try to fight off their murderers and sometimes they do not. But even when the victims attempt to fight back, it is often a lost cause. Why? Because quite often the murderers so far outnumber the victims that the victims do not have a chance. This is particularly true when an entire nation attempts to destroy one segment of its population. Also, oftentimes the murderers have most, if not all, of the weapons. Finally, since the victims are often unaware of the other group's plan to destroy them, the victims are easily led to their own slaughter.

Genocide has taken place throughout history. Historical records from ancient Greece and Rome talk about genocidal acts. So does the Bible. During the Middle Ages genocide occurred during the religious battles of the crusades. Genocide also took place when countries like England, Spain, and France went out and colonized new lands. The American settlers of the West also committed genocidal acts against the Indians. So genocide is a human rights violation that has plagued humanity for a long time.

However, people of the twentieth century like to think that they are more civilized than their ancestors. This is the century, they point out, in which humanity split the atom and put a man on the moon. Nevertheless, some of the worst acts of genocide in the history of humanity have taken place during the twentieth century.

Over three times as many people have been killed in genocidal acts from 1900 to the present as in all of the wars during this century. That is astounding when you realize that over 35 million people have died since 1900 in World War I and II, various civil wars and revolutions. But over 119 million people have died in genocidal acts.

One hundred and nineteen million is a huge number. It is such a large number that it may be hard to imagine. But think of it in these terms. There are about 230 million people in the United States. Thus, to kill 119 million people would be like killing off every single person in every state that borders either the Atlantic or Pacific Ocean. That would include people in all of the following states: Maine, New Hampshire, Massachusetts, Rhode Island, Connecticut, New York, New Jersey, Delaware, Virginia, North Carolina, South Carolina, Georgia, Florida, Washington, Oregon, California. It would also include all of the people living in Washington, D.C. Imagine what it would be like to fly to one of those states and not see a single person alive in the airport, or on any street, or in any store or home in any city or town.

Genocidal Acts in the Twentieth Century
Genocidal acts in this century have taken place in various parts of the world. These have included Europe. Asia, Africa, South America, and Central America.

The first recorded genocidal act of the twentieth century took place in 1904 in southern Africa. A German general named von Throtha issued an order to his troops to slaughter a tribe of people called the Herero. The Germans were trying to set up colonies, and wanted the Hereros out of the way. Not only were the Hereros shot, but their water holes were also poisoned. Out of a population of 80,000 over 60,000 Hereros were murdered.

The most recent act of genocide may have begun in the early 1980s in Iran. The Iranian government may have plans, though no one outside of Iran is absolutely positive, to wipe out a group of people called the Bahá'ís.

The Bahá'ís are members of a religion called Bahá'í. They are a very peaceful people who do not believe in the use of violence. They also do not take part in politics. They believe in the development of good character and want to see the end

94

of prejudice in the world. Nevertheless, the Iranian leaders falsely claim that the Bahá'í religion is "wicked."

Because of their prejudice and hatred of the Bahá'ís, the Iranian officials have denied the Bahá'ís many of their basic human rights. For example, they have destroyed the Bahá'ís' homes, crops, and animals. They have also torn down many of the Bahá'ís' religious shrines and have turned others into parking lots.

Furthermore, the Bahá'ís are no longer allowed to bury their dead in their holy cemeteries. Children of the Bahá'ís have all been expelled from school, and some Bahá'ís girls have been kidnapped and forced to marry men of the Muslim faith. Tens of thousands of Bahá'ís have also been fired from their jobs.

The Iranian government has also murdered hundreds of Bahá'ís and jailed thousands of others. Many Bahá'ís who have been jailed have been tortured.

Numerous nations, as well as the United Nations, have protested Iran's actions against the Bahá'ís. But as late as 1989 there was no end in sight to the human rights violations being committed by the Iranian government against the Bahá'ís.

Between 1904 and today, many other acts of genocide have taken place. One act of genocide that is still making tempers flare was the Turkish slaughter of the Armenians back in 1915.

The Armenian Genocide. In 1908 Sultan Abdul-Hamid II, the ruler of the Ottoman Empire, was forced by his subjects (who included Turks, Arabs, Kurds, Jews, and Armenians) to share his power. A group called the Young Turks immediately assumed the new leadership position and promised a better and fairer way of life for everyone. This made the Armenians extremely thankful. Why? Because between 1894 and 1896 the sultan had ordered the murder of about two hundred thousand Armenians. Thus, under the new leadership the Armenians felt that they would be safe from such acts of violence.

But within one year the new leaders began to break their promises. The first major sign that the Young Turk government was not going to be any fairer than the sultan's was when twenty thousand Armenians were slaughtered in 1909. The new government blamed the sultan and expelled him from his position, but there is proof that the followers of the Young Turks participated in the massacre.

The Young Turks quickly became dictators and started planning ways to rid the Ottoman Empire of the Armenians. They desired to do this for one main reason: They wanted to create a nation in which only Turkish people lived. They believed that in this way they could rule themselves and not worry about the desires and interests of other nationalities. Such a plan, of course, excluded the Armenians who had lived in this region for over three thousand years.

By the time World War I broke out in 1914, the plan to get rid of the Armenians was well under way. At this time the Turks joined with Germany and fought against Czarist Russia, Britain, and France. Different groups of Armenians happened to live in both the Ottoman Empire and Russia, as well as in other areas. And because the Armenians lived in both the Ottoman Empire and in enemy territory, the Turkish leaders came to dislike and distrust the Armenians even more than before. Conveniently, they used this situation as an excuse to carry out their plan to exterminate the Armenians. One government report on this plan read as follows:

> It is a must that the Armenian people be completely exterminated. Not even one single Armenian should be

left on our soil. Even the name "Armenian" should be wiped out. The world is at war. There is no better time than this. No other nation will bother us. Even if they do, the annihilation will become a fact.

From the outset of the genocide, the Turks wanted to prevent the Armenians from fighting back. So before the Armenians knew what was happening, the Young Turks ordered all of them to turn in their weapons. Even those Armenians who did not own weapons went out and bought some in order to have something to turn in. This they did because they were afraid if they did not turn some weapons in they would be accused of being uncooperative and disloyal. They were also afraid of being massacred again as their relatives and fellow Armenians had been in the 1890s and in 1909.

Once all of the weapons had been turned in, the Turks killed one thousand Armenian leaders. This was done in order to prevent them from organizing an army to fight

The beginning of the Turkish deportation of the Armenians—May 1915— is shown.

97

against the Turks. The arrest of their leaders terrified the other Armenians and made most of them freeze with fear. They did not know what to do or whom to turn to.

Then the Turks rounded up most of the Armenian men and began killing them. Finally, all of the women, children, elderly, and sick were forced to march into the desert. There, many of them were either beaten or starved to death.

Many people witnessed what the Turks did to the Armenians. One person who saw the slaughter reported the following:

> The streets were filled with bodies of Armenians. Everytime an Armenian went out of doors he was instantly killed. Even very old men and those who were blind and crippled were killed. I saw piles of Armenians in the fields along the road. I saw two ditches filled with corpses of Armenians. There were about 400 in each ravine, mostly men. Another ravine was filled with bodies of little children. I saw a large number of bodies floating down a river.

Prior to 1914, more than two million Armenians lived in the Ottoman Empire. By 1918, after the extermination had taken place, only about one hundred thousand Armenians were left.

As previously stated, the Turks not only aimed to kill all the Armenians but also wanted to wipe out every last trace that they had ever lived. The Turks tried to accomplish that by various methods. They burned down and destroyed all of the Armenians' churches and cultural monuments. They took their land and homes and gave them to other people. Any Armenian children who were not killed were taken from their parents, given new names, and raised by Turks.

While this was taking place, many countries threatened to

punish all members of the Turkish government who planned or carried out the killings. But they did not do anything else to actually halt the genocide. And after the war, they all seemed to forget about their promises to punish the guilty Turks. In fact, almost everyone except the remaining Armenians seemed to forget that the slaughter had ever taken place. That is the main reason why the extermination of the Armenians has been called "the forgotten genocide."

At the end of World War I, a new Turkish government came to power and trials were held for a few of the people who were responsible for the mass murder of the Armenians. Those people were found guilty and punished; however, most of those who were responsible were never tried in court. Others escaped from Turkey, but nobody tried to track them down. As a result, very few of the guilty were ever punished.

Also, nothing was ever done to repay the Armenians for what happened to them and their relatives. Neither their land nor their homes were ever given back to them. Those Armenians who had escaped the killings by fleeing to other nations were not invited back to their old country.

Furthermore, the government of Turkey did everything it could to prevent any discussion of the Armenian genocide. It simply wanted to forget what had happened.

But as previously mentioned, the Turkish genocide of the Armenians is still a heated issue today. The current Turkish government absolutely refuses to admit that the genocidal act ever took place. It continues to spend huge amounts of money and time to get rid of any mention of the Armenian slaughter in films and books. The officials in the Turkish government simply do not want people to think about the crimes their ancestors committed.

For over seventy years Armenians have called upon the Turkish people to admit that their countrymen committed the genocide. At the very least, the Armenians living today want an apology from the Turkish government. But it does not seem as if that is going to happen in the near future.

A small group of Armenians living outside of Turkey is so furious about the Turkish government's behavior that it has been trying to seek revenge. Since 1973 Armenian terrorists have killed over twenty-six Turkish diplomats. This is a classic example of how an event long ago in history can still have a strong impact on people living today who had nothing to do with it.

These people are survivors of the Armenian slaughter by the Turks.

Many people claim that the guilty Turks should have been hunted down and punished. In that way, they say, all of the other nations in the world would have seen that those who commit genocide do not get away with it. But that did not happen.

The Holocaust. Less than twenty-five years later the Nazis began their planned extermination of all of the Jewish people on earth. That crime against humanity has been named the Holocaust. The word "holocaust" means "a thorough destruction by fire." Thus, the Holocaust refers to the fact that millions of Jewish people were either burned alive or burned to ashes after being gassed to death.

Adolf Hitler, the leader of Germany, hated Jewish people with a passion. He conjured up all sorts of lies about them and convinced other people that they were facts. For instance, he blamed the Jewish people for Germany's loss in World War I. He also accused them of destroying Germany's economy. Hitler simply could not accept the truth for Germany's problems and ended up blaming innocent people.

Hitler's "dream" was to have Germany rule the world. But he believed that before that could happen the German people would have to become a "pure race." He simply meant that he did not want anybody around at all who was different from the "average" German. This attitude led to his decision to kill the Jews. At the same time he also planned to kill other people who were also "different"—people like the Gypsies and the mentally and physically handicapped.

In order to get the German people to share his "dream," Hitler appealed to anti-Semitic (showing hatred against Jewish people) attitudes which had been deeply rooted in their culture for generations. He did everything he could to make them believe that Jewish people were less than human. Beginning in the early 1930s Hitler made speech after speech about "the evil ways" of the Jews. He even had such lies taught in the German schools. After the Germans lost World War II and the Holocaust came to an end, one German concentration camp guard said: "Every third word we heard, even back in grammar school, was about how the Jews were to blame for everything and how they ought to be weeded out. It was hammered into us that this would only be for the good of our people. . . . We weren't supposed to think for ourselves."

Hitler also hired young German thugs to force Jews to pick up garbage and wash the streets. Other German officials held book burnings at which books by Jewish authors were destroyed.

In 1935 the Germans passed the Nuremberg Laws. These laws stated that Jewish people were no longer German citizens. As a result, German Jews no longer had the same rights as other German citizens.

Throughout this time the democratic nations of the world were, for the most part, silent about how the Germans were mistreating the Jews. Some nations felt that loud protests would just cause more grief for the Jews. Others simply did not care about their fate.

This silence, however, only encouraged Hitler to carry out his plans for ridding the earth of Jews. Recalling the Turkish slaughter of the Armenians, Hitler said, "Who still talks nowadays of the extermination of the Armenians?" Hitler meant that he could probably kill the Jews and get away with it because other nations would not do anything to stop him.

Eastern European countries where citizens had long hated Jews also began taking the Jews' human rights away. These were countries like Poland, Romania, Lithuania, and Latvia.

By the time Germany started World War II in 1939, it already controlled many countries in Europe. In each of these nations the Jews were deprived of their freedom. As mentioned earlier they were forced to wear yellow Stars of David so that everyone would know that they were Jews. This not only made them stand out, but it also made them seem like they were different or odd. All of this brought about great brutality. For example, many non-Jews frequently called the Jews cruel names, spit on them, and beat them.

At the same time, Jews were also made to obey a curfew. In doing so, they were told when they could and could not go outside. They were also fired from their jobs and kicked out of schools. Signs with cruel messages about Jews were posted in cities. Some said BEWARE OF JEWS AND PICKPOCKETS. These signs sent messages to non-Jews that Jews were no better than criminals. Many of the Jewish places of worship were also destroyed.

In many of these countries the Jews were ripped from their homes and forced into places called ghettos. These were large areas in cities where the Jews were cooped up like animals. In the ghetto they were immediately put on a starvation diet. Each day they were only given a tiny bit of bread, potatoes, and fat.

The Jews were neither allowed to leave the ghettos nor communicate with anybody outside of them. If a Jew got too close to the entrance of the ghetto then he or she was often shot and killed. Many of the Jews were also forced to do slave labor.

Then in 1941 the Nazi slaughter of the Jews began. At first the Jews were rounded up and shot on the spot, and then dumped into mass graves. One woman, Rivka, narrowly survived under these exact circumstances. Speaking of her ordeal she said:

> We were rounded up, stripped of our clothing, and
> led into the forest to a large open pit. Then they began

to shoot us in the back of the head. Men, women, children, all were shot. My husband . . . my two little children. . . . I felt a sudden sting in the back of the head and fell into the pit. The bullet must have grazed me. There were dead bodies below me and on top of me. I remained very quiet; it was hard to breathe. Then the shooting and murdering stopped. It was dark. I could still hear gasps from the bodies. I worked my way to the top and fled into the forest. I was found by resistance fighters, and they took care of me. After the war I made my way to Israel.

Other methods were also used. Many large groups of Jews were drowned, while others were burned to death. Still others were forced inside the back of enclosed trucks and gassed to death.

But the Nazis found all of these methods too slow and expensive. As a result, they began to develop faster and more efficient ways of murdering.

By 1942 the Nazis began moving Jews to the new death camps that had been designed. The main death camps were set up in Poland. Jews from almost all over Europe were sent to these camps. Many people were sent hundreds and even thousands of miles from the ghettos or their homes. The Nazis had one reason and only one reason for shipping the Jews to the death camps—to murder them.

The Nazis did not tell the Jews that they were being shipped to death camps but tricked them into believing that they were being sent to labor camps. These lies helped to keep the Jews under control and from rebelling.

The train trips to the death camps were nightmarish. Hundreds upon hundreds of men, women, and children were crammed so tightly into cattle cars that they found it next to impossible to stretch out, let alone move about. Many died before they even got to the death camps. Some were crushed to death, while others starved to death.

A French guide shows a U.S. Army officer the crematory where the bodies of Jewish, French, Russian, and Slav slave laborers were cremated in a Nazi concentration camp.

As soon as the Jews arrived at the death camps, the Nazis made the decision as to which Jews would immediately die, and which ones would become slave laborers until the time that they would be sent to death. Because of all of the confusion and fear, most of the Jews did not know what was going on.

Those who were going to be killed were told to take off their clothes and get ready for a shower. They were then led to huge rooms with signs that said BATHS. Inside were shower nozzles. Sometimes the Jews were even handed a piece of soap and a towel. As soon as the room was packed with hundreds of people, huge doors were slammed shut. Then the gas, which shot out of the "shower" nozzles, was turned on. It usually took up to ten minutes for everyone to die.

Even after the Jews were dead they were not left alone. The bodies had their gold teeth knocked out, and their hair shaved. The Nazis melted down the gold, and used the mounds of hair for things like stuffing pillows.

Next the bodies were burned in the huge furnaces. The ashes were either dumped into ditches or rivers. Oftentimes the remaining bones were crushed and used as fertilizer. Other times the fat on the bodies was used to make soap.

The Nazis were extremely proud of their murderous accomplishments. Many actually bragged that each of their death camps could kill many thousands of people a day. Heinrich Himmler, a Nazi leader, even said, "We have written a glorious page in our history. We have taken everything they [the Jews] owned."

Elie Wiesel, a survivor of the Holocaust, knows how true Himmler's words were. Now a famous writer, Wiesel has written that:

> The Nazis' aim was to make the Jewish universe
> shrink—from town to neighborhood, from neighborhood

to street, from street to house, from house to room, from room to garret, from garret to cattle car, from cattle car to gas chamber. And they did the same to the individual—separated from his or her community, then from his or her family, then from his or her identity, eventually becoming a work permit, then a number, until the number was turned into ashes.

The lives of those Jews who were forced to be slave laborers were almost unbelievable. All day and night they were forced to smell the burning flesh of their fellow Jews. They lived in filthy barracks that were swarming with fleas and rats. And not only were they almost starved to death, but they were also frequently beaten by the Nazis guards.

Whenever a person became too weak or sick to work then he or she was killed. So, each and every day those who managed to hang on to life had to watch silently as their fellow inmates were slaughtered. The average prisoner only lived about three months before he or she either died or was killed.

The Holocaust has been called "the most horrible crime against humanity in the history of the world." There are several reasons for that claim. One, more people were killed in that one genocidal act than ever before. Two, no other genocidal act had been so carefully planned and carried out. Not only were special death factories built, but the Nazis kept daily, weekly, and monthly charts of how many people were killed. They also developed a special process of killing that was run like an assembly line in a factory. Three, this was the first genocidal act in which modern technology was used. For instance, the Nazis developed new and more powerful types of gas to use in their gas chambers so they could increase the number of Jews they killed each day. Four, the Nazis used experts in the area of medicine, engineering, architecture, and other fields in order to carry out their act of genocide. Fifth, the German people who planned and carried out such atrocities were not ignorant barbarians. Actually they were just the opposite. Many were extremely intelligent and sophisticated. Their fellow citizens and ancestors had created some of the greatest literature, music, and art the world has ever known. Over the years that has made some people in other countries ask themselves, "Under certain circumstances would we also be capable of committing similar atrocities?"

People often wonder whether the Jews tried to fight back. Thousands did fight back while millions did not. As for those who did, many held armed revolts in the ghettos. The most famous of these was the battle in the Warsaw Ghetto. Others fought the Nazis in the death camps. On one occasion the Jews actually blew up one of the gas chambers in the Auschwitz camp. Another group revolted in Sobibor death camp, and up to three hundred or more prisoners escaped. Many Jews also joined armies of resistance that fought the Nazis.

Victims of the Nazi concentration camp at Belsen are shown in a mass grave.

Other Jews tried to flee from the Nazis by moving to other nations. Many of these people successfully escaped, but many others were either caught or sent back to German territory by the nations they fled to.

However, it is also true that millions of Jews went quietly to their deaths. There were several reasons for this. First, before the slaughter even began the Nazis did everything they possibly could to frighten and weaken the Jews. The Nazis did this in many different ways. They used propaganda to make whole nations of people hate the Jews. The Nazis constantly wrote and broadcast statements like this: "When Jewish blood drips from the knife, then things are twice as good." The Nazis also humiliated the Jews by making them outcasts.

Second, even though there were rumors going around about the death camps, nobody really believed them. Who, in their right mind, could believe that millions of people were being slaughtered just because they were of a certain religious faith?

Third, as previously mentioned, the Nazis never told the Jews that they were being shipped to death camps. Instead, the Jews were told that they were being sent to labor camps in order to help Germany's war effort.

Fourth, the Nazis starved the Jews in both the ghettos and the death camps. As a result, many Jews died of starvation and various diseases. Others became too weak to fight against the Nazis.

Fifth, the Nazis attacked towns so quickly that the Jews did not have time to get organized. This made it impossible for the Jews to really put up a good fight.

Another question that people often ask is this: "Didn't anyone else try to help the Jews?" Some people did, but most did not. Generally speaking, the world was silent as the Nazis slaughtered the Jews.

Most of the people in Eastern Europe were anti-Semitic and detested the Jews as much as Hitler. Some caring people in those countries did try to help the Jews, but they could not do enough to stop the Holocaust.

Some of the freer nations in Western Europe did a lot to help the Jews. The country that did the most was Denmark.

The king of Denmark, who was not a Jew, cared deeply about helping the Jews. He said, "If the Germans want the Jews in Denmark to wear the yellow star then I and my whole family will wear it." That was his way of protesting against the unfair treatment of the Jews by the Nazis.

Then in 1943 the Nazis ordered Denmark to ship all of its Jewish citizens, about eight thousand in all, to death camps. The Danish citizens immediately tried to rescue as many Jews as possible; and within a short amount of time, the Danes actually smuggled seven thousand Jews to freedom.

As for the United States, it did too little too late to help the Jews. For many years it refused to allow the Jewish victims to escape to the United States. Along with England, the United States also refused to bomb death camps. When the United States finally did try to help, most of the Jews had already been slaughtered.

It is certainly true that during this time the United States was fighting for its survival in World War II. Nevertheless, some historians now claim that the United States could have done much more to help the Jews without jeopardizing the war effort.

At the end of the war (between 1945 and 1946) an international military court met in Nuremberg, Germany, to conduct a trial of twenty-two former Nazi leaders for the crimes they had committed. The judges were from the United States, Great Britain, France, and the Soviet Union.

By the time of the trial many Nazi leaders had already

changed their names and gone into hiding. Thus, it was impossible to prosecute them at that time.

Among the crimes the former Nazis were charged with were "crimes against humanity." These crimes included murder, extermination, enslavement, and other inhumane acts. The Nazis claimed that when they murdered the Jews they were just following Hitler's orders. The judges did not accept that as an excuse. Nineteen out of the twenty-two former Nazis were found guilty. Twelve of them were executed. The rest were given prison sentences.

Since 1946 many other former Nazis leaders have been hunted down. After being tried, most have been found guilty and have been punished. Still others are going through trials today or are being hunted down so they can be brought to trial.

UN Genocide Convention
Even after the Nuremberg Trials, many in the world were not through worrying about genocide. As previously mentioned, many were so disturbed by the Holocaust that in 1948 the United Nations adopted the UN Declaration of Human Rights (see chap. 2).

But even before that, every member of the United Nations voted in favor of making genocide "a crime under international law." That was on December 11, 1946. Never before had nations across the world taken such a stance. The UN General Assembly also declared that everything possible should be done to prevent genocide from taking place again.

Then on December 9, 1948, the UN General Assembly adopted the Genocide Convention. It was the first of many human rights treaties to be adopted by the UN.

The convention makes genocide an international crime. It states that to kill national, ethnic, racial, or religious groups or members of those groups is against international law. It also declares that genocide is a crime whether it is committed in peacetime or during war. The hope was to prevent another tragedy similar to the Holocaust.

By signing the convention a nation agrees to try to prevent genocide. It also agrees to help punish those individuals or nations that commit genocidal acts.

For over thirty-five years the United States refused to sign the Genocide Convention. Some senators felt that if the United States signed it, it would allow other nations to interfere with different U.S. policies. On the other hand, almost every president from Harry S. Truman to Ronald Reagan wanted the United States to sign the convention. However, it is also true that most presidents were so involved with other work that getting the convention approved in Congress was not their number one priority.

Over that thirty-five-year period many people stated that the United States could not be a truly effective fighter for the protection of other people's human rights until it had signed the convention. This was because some countries could claim (and did claim) that if the United States really cared about human rights it would have signed the Genocide Convention. Finally, after years of debate in Congress, the United States signed the Genocide Convention in 1985.

What About Mass Political Killings? It is very important to note that the Genocide Convention excludes some types of mass killings from its definition of genocide. In the present form of the convention, genocide refers to any of the following acts committed with the intent to destroy, in whole or in part, a national ethnic, racial or religious group such as (a) killing members of the group, (b) causing serious bodily harm to members of the group, (c) deliberately inflicting on the group conditions of life calculated to bring about its physical

112

destruction in whole or in part, (d) imposing measures intended to prevent births within the group, and (e) forcibly transferring children of the group to another group.

By this definition the current Genocide Convention does not consider mass political killings to be acts of genocide. Mass political killings are carried out for many different reasons. The most common reason, though, is because one group (usually government officials) often greatly disagrees with the political beliefs of another group and does not trust the group. Such killings often result in the deaths of thousands or even tens of thousands or millions of people. In the very recent past, mass killings have been committed by such governments as Argentina, El Salvador, Guatemala, Indonesia, Kampuchea (formerly known as Cambodia), and Uganda.

In some countries the police carry out such killings, while in others soldiers often perform them. Or sometimes

Here lie the skulls of thousands of victims of the Khmer Rouge.

113

governments set up "death squads" to murder their opponents. Death squads are often made up of both off-duty police and military personnel.

The purposes and results of such killings are basically the same as those that are defined by the Genocide Convention as being cases of genocide. The killings are also generally carried out according to a plan and are conducted in a systematic way. Furthermore, the method of killing is just as brutal: people are shot, beaten to death, and drowned.

In Uganda so many bodies were dumped into a river that it turned red from all of the blood. Entire villages of people have been massacred in Uganda, and mass graves have been uncovered in Argentina and Kampuchea.

Common sense tells one that such mass murders are definitely examples of genocide. Why, then, are mass political murders not considered to be genocidal acts by the Genocide Convention?

During the initial debates about the treaty, the Soviet Union representatives said that they did not believe political massacres were examples of genocidal acts, and thus should not be included in the convention's definition. One reason that they might have said that is because the Soviet Union had committed numerous political massacres in the 1930s and 1940s. Some historians claim that the Soviet Union was probably trying to avoid being accused of having committed genocide by eliminating political killings from the definition.

Some countries agreed with the Soviet Union, and some did not. After many long debates the various countries in the UN still disagreed over whether political killings were examples of genocide or not. Thus, a weak compromise was worked out. It was decided that "political massacres" would not be included in the Genocide Convention's definition of genocide. At the time it was thought if the compromise had not been worked out that certain nations, including the Soviet Union, would not have signed the convention. If that had happened then the convention would not have been ratified or formally approved.

Genocide Still Continues. By 1988 ninety-seven nations had ratified the Genocide Convention. That included every major nation in the world and every democratic country. And yet, genocide continues to take place throughout the world. Since 1948 at least a dozen cases of genocide have occurred.

One of the most recent acts of genocide occurred in Kampuchea between 1975 and 1979. At least two million people were slaughtered in a country with only seven million citizens. Mass graves were later discovered that contained over eight thousand bodies. The killings have been described as a bloodbath, and some have referred to Kampuchea as a "killing field."

After a long civil war, Kampuchea was taken over by a revolutionary communist group called the Khmer Rouge. The Khmer Rouge wanted to develop a totally new type of society—a society in which everyone farmed and shared everything that they owned or made. To accomplish that, they started by forcing hundreds of thousands of city people to march long distances out into the countryside. Even crippled children, pregnant women, and very ill hospital patients were made to join the march. Thousands of people either died or were killed by Khmer Rouge along the way. The roads were littered with corpses, and nobody was allowed to bury the dead.

Once the people were in the country they were forced to do hard labor many hours a day—from before sunrise to after sunset. Again, many thousands of people either died or were killed by the Khmer Rouge.

At this time the Khmer Rouge began executing all of the

leaders, officials, and soldiers from the previous government. They wanted to weed out all of their enemies. But the killing did not stop there. By 1976 the Khmer Rouge were murdering anyone with an education—scholars, teachers, and even young elementary- and high-school students. The Khmer Rouge did not want anyone around who had been influenced by the previous government. Sometimes entire villages were wiped out.

In 1976 *Time* magazine reported that

> In a typical incident hundreds of former army officers were bound hand and foot, loaded onto trucks, and machine-gunned on the outskirts of town.
>
> [Survivors] tell tales of people being clubbed to death "to save ammunition." Others have been bound together and buried alive by bulldozers, or suffocated by having plastic bags tied over their heads.

Why was nothing done by other nations to stop this? Especially by those countries that had signed the Genocide Convention? The simple fact is, many people did not believe that the mass murder was really taking place. And as for those countries that did believe they were taking place, they did nothing more than issue protests. But that did not do any good, because the killings continued to go on each and every day.

The Value of the Genocide Convention. One must wonder whether the Genocide Convention has served any worthwhile purpose at all. Is the world any better off with it or not? And why has the Genocide Convention not succeeded in bringing about a total end to genocidal acts?

The answer to the first question is that the world is only somewhat better off. First, many more people are concerned about stopping genocide today than they were in the past.

The genocidal slaughter committed by the Khmer Rouge in Kampuchea resulted in mass graves.

117

Second, those countries that have signed the Genocide Convention know that they can be punished, and that may have prevented them from committing genocide. Third, the United Nations may have helped to prevent certain genocidal massacres from taking place. How? By putting its peacekeeping troops in many nations that were about to commit human rights violations, the UN may have staved off such situations. The UN has also kept a close eye on nations that have been suspected of being on the verge of committing genocide, and warned such countries against doing so.

Nevertheless, millions of people have been slaughtered since the ratification of the Genocide Convention. Why?

There are many reasons for this. First, not all of the nations in the world have signed the Genocide Convention. Of course, if a nation has not signed the convention then it is not lawfully bound to follow it. As a result, the leaders of some of these nations believe that they can commit genocide and not worry about being punished. Sometimes that is exactly what happens.

Second, the Genocide Convention is more concerned with punishing those who commit genocide than it is with trying to prevent genocidal acts from taking place. This is true in that it does not outline any sound ideas on how the world can prevent genocide. That is a major weakness of the convention. As Dr. Leo Kuper, an expert on genocide, has stated, "Punishment after the act does not address the problem of preventing loss of life."

Third, though the convention calls for the punishment of those who commit genocide, it does not outline how a person or nation should be punished. Furthermore, an international court has not been established yet. And without such a court there is no place to conduct trials for those who are guilty of committing genocide.

Fourth, as previously mentioned, the Genocide Convention does not consider political massacres to be acts of genocide. This makes the convention much less valuable than it could otherwise be. In effect, this omission conveys the message that nations can kill off its political opponents and not be held responsible for doing so.

Because of these various weaknesses in the convention, Dr. Kuper has called it "almost a dead letter." A "dead letter" is something that has lost its force of authority without being formally done away with. Kuper has also claimed that the UN seems to have a rather weak commitment to ridding the world of genocide.

Does that mean that nothing can ever be done to prevent genocide from taking place? And does it mean that most governments or individuals who commit genocide will continue to get away with it and not be punished?

The answer to both questions is no. It is always possible that the UN could decide to do more to prevent genocide. How? It could revise the convention in order to include mass political killings under its definition of genocide. It could also establish an international court in which to try people who commit acts of genocide. And, it could work out detailed methods for preventing genocide.

These are all ideas for the future. But there are many people around the world who have already developed organizations and are working on plans on how to prevent genocide, and/or punish those who commit genocide.

Dr. Kuper is one of the key people working on the prevention of genocide. He has started an organization called International Alert. Its purpose is to bring information about threats of genocide and actual massacres to the attention of the world so that they might act to halt them.

Dr. Israel Charny, an expert on genocide, is another person who is trying to develop a method for preventing genocide. He and his colleagues are currently developing the Early Warning Genocide System. Its purpose will be to keep a constant eye out for possible acts of genocide taking place in the world. If it discovers any acts about to occur or actually taking place, then it would broacast that to the citizens and governments of the world and urge that preventive action be taken.

As for punishing those who commit genocide, Mr. Peter Benenson (the human rights activist who founded Amnesty International, the international human rights organization awarded the Nobel Prize for peace in 1977) has come up with an original idea. He thinks that an international organization should start collecting evidence of genocidal acts, and that such information should be presented at the future trials of those people and nations who commit such crimes. The trials would be like the Nuremberg Trials that were held for the Nazi killers of the Jewish people.

Benenson hopes that since countries would know that such evidence is being collected it would prevent them from committing genocide. Why? Because the countries' political and military leaders might be fearful of being punished.

When all is said and done, maybe the most significant and important effort of all will be the action of individual citizens. Citizens like you, your parents, and your teachers can have a real effect.

That can be accomplished by not ignoring rumors that genocide is taking place. It can be done by urging the UN to revise its Genocide Convention so that it is stronger. It can be done by urging one's leaders to do all they can to prevent genocide and to punish those who commit it. It can be done by educating oneself about genocide. Finally, it can be done by supporting those organizations that are working to rid genocide from the face of the earth.

The sooner all of this happens the more likely it will be that fewer people will become the victims of genocide. If the people of the world do not take on such responsibility then they, too, will be partially responsible and guilty for the genocidal acts. Why? Because "the only thing necessary for the triumph of evil is for good [people] to do nothing."

5

Political Prisoners

Over one million political prisoners are being held by one hundred or more nations today. They can be found in labor camps, jails, torture chambers, and mental hospitals.

Do not let the word "prisoner" fool you. These are not the type of prisoners we usually think of. These prisoners have not harmed anyone, nor have they committed murder. They also have not robbed or stolen anything. Neither have they spied on a country nor given away their country's secrets.

These are special prisoners. They are men, women, and children who are in jail for their political or religious beliefs. Some have been imprisoned because they dared to question or challenge certain actions of their governments. Still others have lost their freedom simply because of their color, race, ethnic background, or nationality.

Their imprisonment violates the Universal Declaration of Human Rights because in each of these situations these individuals had at least one of their basic human rights taken away. And that is why they are called political prisoners.

If a political prisoner has not used or suggested the use of

123

This political prisoner was jailed by the former Marcos government in the
Philippines.

violence, then he or she is often referred to as a "prisoner of conscience." By following his or her conscience, such a person acts in a way that he or she believes is morally right and accepts the responsibility for doing so. The term "prisoner of conscience" was coined by Amnesty International.

The Plight of Political Prisoners

Have you or anybody you know ever been punished for worshiping in a church, synagogue, or other holy place? Plenty of people have in other parts of the world. Do you know anybody who has ever been arrested solely because of the color of his or her skin? At this very moment that is actually happening in several parts of the world. Have you ever heard of anyone who has ever been arrested because of something he or she wrote or said? In some nations that happens quite frequently. Have your parents or any of their friends been arrested and/or tortured for belonging to a labor union? Probably not, but it is not uncommon in many nations.

Let us look at the stories of some people who have experienced such situations. In that way you will begin to get a better idea of how fragile certain human rights are in various parts of the world.

Take the case of Aleksandr Argentov, a Christian living in the Soviet Union. At the age of twenty-five, Aleksandr was incarcerated in a mental hospital and given drugs that caused him incredible pain. His "crime"? Being a Christian. The Soviet government said that his belief in God and the Christian religion was a sign of mental illness.

The Soviet officials think that being religious is a sign of insanity because they do not believe God exists. They want all of their citizens to be atheists—people who deny the existence of God.

But there are millions of people in Russia who believe in

God. They are Christians, Jews, and Muslims, and many of them are constantly ill-treated because of their faith and beliefs.

The Soviet Union is not the only communist nation that tries to deny its people freedom of religion. Other communist nations either strongly limit or ban many religious activities. Most of these nations frown upon their people being religious, and as a result many nations often mistreat their religious citizens. These include such nations as Albania, China, Vietnam, Czechoslovakia, and Kampuchea.

Many non-Communist countries also mistreat their people because of their religious beliefs, but the leaders in these countries generally do not frown upon all religions. They may favor one religion over another, or they may distrust the followers of a particular religion. If that is the case then a country may ban that particular religion, or it might mistreat its members. In the recent past that has happened in Iran, Cameroon, Chile, Turkey, and Libya.

Why do certain countries deny religious freedom? Some government officials feel that certain religious groups interfere with the nation's problems. How? The religious groups may help the poor, or call on the government to be fairer to its people. Some get involved in peace activities such as marches and rallies. The governments often resent such activities and punish the religious groups involved.

To deny someone his or her religious freedom is a violation of Article 18 of the Universal Declaration of Human Rights. That article states, in part, that "Everyone has the right to freedom of religion. . . ." It could not be more simply stated, but the lack of religious freedom accounts for much of the human rights abuse in the world today.

Racism and prejudice have also resulted in other types of human rights violations. (For a detailed discussion of these

126

situations, see chap. 3.) One such violation involved Bessie Nobathembu Fihla, a twenty-year-old black student who lives in South Africa. She was recently arrested and tortured, but she is not exactly sure why since the police never charged her with a crime.

While in prison, the guards hooked a hood tightly around her head. Then they burned her with electric shocks.

As far as Bessie knows her "crime" could be that she has black skin. A lot of people in South Africa are arrested for that reason. Or it might have been because she belonged to a group that is opposed to South Africa's racist policies, called apartheid. As you have read, these are policies that give white people almost absolute power over black people.

By mistreating Bessie in this way South Africa violated Articles 5, 7, and 9 of the declaration. Article 5 states that no one shall be tortured. Article 7 says, "All are equal before the law and are entitled without any discrimination to equal protection of the law." Article 9 asserts that "No one shall be subjected to arbitrary arrest . . ." This means that government officials need to have a real cause or a good reason to arrest someone, and should not simply do it because they dislike or disagree with a person.

Recep Marasli, a citizen of Turkey, is also a political prisoner. He is currently serving nineteen years in prison because he wrote numerous articles and books on political subjects that the Turkish government did not approve of. That was it. Nothing more.

Such treatment by the Turkish government is clearly in violation of Article 19 of the declaration. It is the one that declares that "Everyone has the right to freedom of opinion and expression."

There are many other governments that treat their citizens like Turkey does. They, too, do everything they can to control what their citizens write, read, or speak about. Furthermore, they do not like it when their citizens complain about or criticize the government. Quite often these governments will seriously punish those who do so.

A person like Recep Marasli is often called a dissident. A dissident is one who has a difference of opinion with one's government and expresses that opinion either orally or in writing. A dissident who is arrested becomes a political prisoner.

Here is yet another story of a dissident. Dr. Ivan Zografski is a seventy-year-old retired doctor, and he was imprisoned for five years in Yugoslavia for criticizing his government.

Dr. Zografski complained about two things. First, he said his country's economy was bad. Basically, all he meant was that food, clothing, and housing cost too much. Second, he stated that the country's leaders were not doing a good job.

Dr. Zografski's complaints were not made to groups of people at meetings or over television, and he was not trying to talk other people into rebelling against the government. Instead, he was simply talking with friends, at various times, in his own home, his friends' homes, and in restaurants.

Dr. Zografski's punishment, however, will not end when he gets out of prison. When he is freed he will not have any property to go back to because the government has confiscated all of it. But even there, his punishment does not end. As soon as he walks out the front door of the prison he is going to be forced to leave his country.

By punishing Dr. Zografski in this way, the Yugoslavian government has violated many articles of the declaration. For instance, it violated Article 17, which states that "Everyone has the right to own property . . ." Among the others it has violated is Article 18, which declares that "Everyone has the right to freedom of thought."

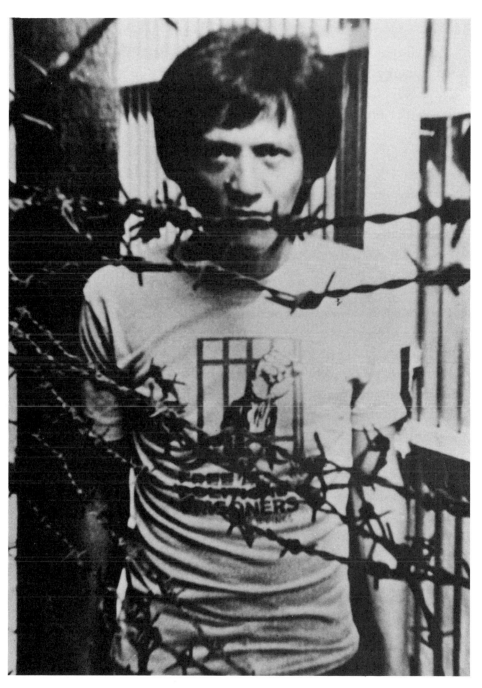

A political prisoner stands imprisoned behind barbed wire.

129

Again, Yugoslavia is not the only country that tries to shut its citizens up in this way. Many other countries are also guilty of doing it.

Now let us take the story of Héctor Solís Saavedra. He was the president of a construction workers' labor union in Chile and was very active in helping his union members gain such rights as fair pay, fair hours, and healthy working conditions.

Suddenly, without warning, he was arrested and tortured. Then he was banished to a tiny village to live. Not only was the village over three hundred miles from his home, but he was forced to live in a shack. This was his government's way of punishing him for being a member of a labor union and working for others' basic human rights.

While Saavedra was in jail, the government accused him of trying to convince workers to go on strike. Workers usually go on strike to gain better pay or working conditions, but government officials claimed that he did this because he wanted the workers to protest government policies. Saavedra denied this, and the government never presented any proof to show that it was right.

By treating Saavedra this way, the Chilean government violated Articles 5, 9, and 23 of the declaration. Articles 5 and 9 are the same ones that South Africa violated in dealing with Bessie Nobathembu Fihla. Article 23 says, in part, that "Everyone has the right to form and to join trade unions . . ." Once again, Chile is not the only nation to punish labor union members in this fashion; many others do as well.

Many people have actually become political prisoners by trying to help others who have been denied their human rights. Most, if not all, of these people knew they were risking their own freedom and safety by assisting others, but they did so anyhow. Why? Because they were following their consciences.

Marianella García Villas was just such a person. María was the president of a human rights organization in El Salvador before she was slain.

In her work, María gathered a great deal of information about how the El Salvadorian government ran death squads. Such information illustrated how people were kidnapped and tortured by the death squads, and then never seen again. It also included facts about how people were shot and killed in the streets.

María was arrested twice because of her human rights work. Both times she was told to quit her work because the government was against it. The second time she was badly beaten.

Then in 1981 she was called "a traitor to the country." María knew that other people who had been called traitors had been killed, and so she immediately left El Salvador.

But María could not bear to let others suffer, and so she returned to El Salvador to obtain more information about the abuse of human rights. She planned to present her findings to the United Nations Commission on Human Rights, but as soon as she returned to her country she was killed.

Killing María was the El Salvadorian government's way of stopping her from telling the truth. It also stopped her from helping other people.

El Salvador violated many of María's human rights. But when it violated Article 3 of the declaration, it took away what most people believe is the most important of all the rights—the right to life."

And once again El Salvador is far from the only nation guilty of such human rights abuse. If a list of such nations were written up, it would be a long one.

131

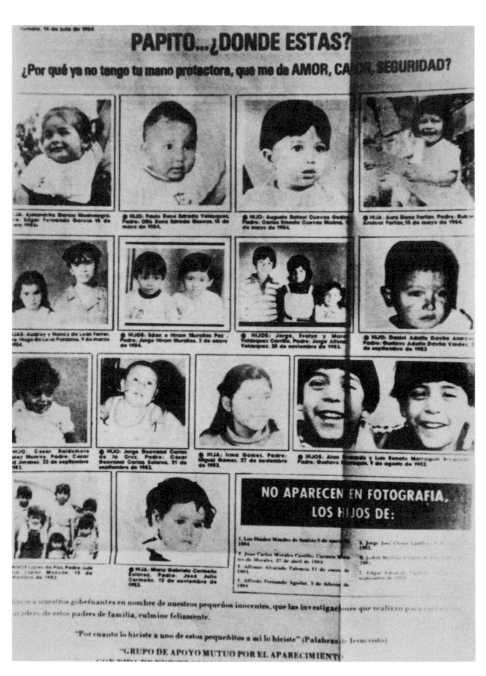

These are photographs of children who "disappeared" in Argentina.

132

Stories such as these raise many questions in the minds of people. One of the questions most frequently asked about political prisoners is this: "Why do people stay in countries that treat their people so poorly?" There are no easy answers, but there are many that do make sense.

Numerous countries simply will not allow their citizens to leave their country without special permission. The catch is, though, that many of these same countries refuse to grant that special permission. As a result, the people who wish to leave are stuck.

There are many reasons why certain countries prevent their citizens from leaving. Some leaders believe that they need as many people as possible in order to keep the nation's industry, economy, and military as strong as possible. Other nations' officials claim that if they allow people to leave, then they (the citizens) may give the nation's secrets to its enemies. Still other governments do not want their critics or opponents to leave because they fear that such people may attack the nation (either with words or weapons) from the outside. Among the nations that have recently refused its citizens the right to leave are the following: Albania, South Africa, Bulgaria, Romania, Hungary, Ethiopia, East Germany, Iran, Russia, Cuba, and China. In one sense, the citizens in these countries are almost like prisoners.

Such countries are guilty of violating Articles 13 and 14 of the declaration. Article 13 states, in part, that "Everyone has the right to leave any country, including their own. . . ." Article 14 asserts that "Everyone has the right to seek and to enjoy in other countries asylum from persecution." That means that if someone is poorly treated in a country, then he or she has every right to leave and the right to seek acceptance in a nonpersecuting country.

On the other hand, some people may not move out of a

country because they are too poor to do so. They may not be able to afford a car or other transportation or even the cost to move their belongings.

Still others might truly love their country. They may hope and believe that situation in their country will soon get better, and that life will soon be enjoyable and safe again.

Then there are many people who think that they will never find themselves in trouble with their governments. They feel that only other people will be poorly treated. But then when they do get in trouble it is often too late to leave because they may already be in prison.

There are always some who wish to leave but have no place to go where it is safe. This may be true because many of the nations that they could get to are just as repressive or even more so.

Finally, some actually do escape. While it means that they may have to learn a new language and/or start all over again in a new type of work, they do have more freedom and are able to enjoy their basic human rights.

People have asked, "Why do some people write and say things in those countries where they know they will be thrown in prison or be tortured?" Still others have asked, "Why do people practice their religion or join organizations when they know they will be punished?"

Again, there are no easy answers to these questions. But maybe this political prisoner has said it best: "When do I act like a human if not now? When do I enjoy my rights if not now? When I'm dead? Then it will be too late. I am a human being. I have rights, and I will enjoy them now! Not five years from now. Not twenty years from now. I may be dead by then."

"If we lose our capacity to be outraged when we see others submitted to atrocities, then we lose our right to call ourselves civilized human beings."

—Vladimir Hertzog, Brazilian journalist who was possibly tortured to death.

6

Torture

The use of torture is so widespread that it has been called "an epidemic in the world." It is reported that torture is used, at least to some extent, by about ninety-eight out of the approximately two hundred countries in the world. And that is true despite the fact that Article 5 of the Universal Declaration of Human Rights declares that "No one shall be subjected to torture or to cruel, inhuman or degrading treatment or punishment."

Torture is not only used in countries ruled by dictators but also by democratic countries. As for its use in democracies, Amnesty International reports that "torture has been used in the twentieth century by the British in Aden, Kenya, and Northern Ireland, and the Americans in Vietnam." Torture victims, both in the past as well as today, have included people of all ages, races, social classes, professions, and religious and political beliefs.

The thought of torture often sends chills through one's body. But what exactly is torture? It could involve burning, shocking, beating, or whipping someone. Or it could mean frightening someone by threatening to beat or kill him or her, forcing someone to watch another person be tortured, or forcing drugs into a person that cause pain to both the body and mind. Amnesty International has pointed out that "Essential to torture is the sense that the torturer controls everything, even life itself."

Many people who have been tortured have spoken out about their experiences. These testimonies by the victims provide a rather detailed picture of the institution of torture.

Mojan Homayousar, a twenty-four-year-old math teacher, was arrested for handing out leaflets that criticized the leader of Iran, Ayatollah Khomeini. "They took me to a remote area," he explains, "and they were going to kill me. I recognized one of the guards and I called his name. He lifted his machete and brought it down hard. I felt nothing. I looked over and they were playing with an object, throwing it to each other. I realized it was my leg."

The Soviet Union has reportedly tortured numerous people for disagreeing with its governmental policies by forcing them to take huge amounts of unprescribed drugs. Such drugs are frequently used to both control a person and/or to cause him or her pain.

A dissident named Leonid Plyusch was given such heavy doses of "medication" that he was in constant agony. "The discomfort," he said, "was so intense that all you could do was endlessly search for a new position" to sit in.

Another Soviet political prisoner, Vladimir Tsurikov, who was also force-fed drugs because he wanted to move to another country, said this: "My legs began to twist about in a ridiculous way. I lost the ability to walk. . . . Fainting fits began, recurring very often; I fell and hit my head. . . . Sometimes I experienced slight shivering and my tongue hung out. This nightmare lasted a week. . . ."

136

Torture is not always something that causes physical pain. Sometimes it consists of actions that torment the mind or emotions. This is called psychological torture. Sometimes political prisoners are forced to watch and/or listen as a loved one is tortured. It is also not unusual that a prisoner be threatened with torture or death if he or she does not confess to something. This is exactly what happened to Lucia Guillermina Morales.

Because Lucia belonged to a workers' union of which the Chilean officials did not approve, she and her daughter were jailed. Then, as Lucia explains, the torture for both of them began. While her daughter suffered physical torture, Lucia suffered mental or psychological torture. "The guards separated us violently," she reports. "Then they took her to another room, and there I listened in horror as they began to torture her with electricity—my own daughter. When I heard her moans, her terrible screams, I couldn't take it any more. I thought I would go mad, that my head and my entire body were going to explode."

Incidents such as these are not random occurrences. Rather, they take place on a fairly frequent basis, and that is because certain governments often see torture as an acceptable method for controlling their citizens.

The use of torture is so frowned upon by most people that those governments that use it will usually deny it. For instance, when questioned about the use of torture in his country, one Chilean official said, "Torture in Chile? It makes me laugh. When I think of torture, I think of the fifteenth century; or the fourteenth century, the Middle Ages. But not Chile, today."

Possibly most think torture is a practice that was only used in the past. But, quite obviously, that is not true. However, it is worth finding out why and how torture was used in the past because in that way one can compare and contrast why and how it is used today. At the same time, one can also try to figure out if the age we live in is any more civilized than past ages when torture was used so frequently.

History of Torture

Although some ancient peoples tortured their enemies, torture was most frequently used as a form of punishment among members of their own group.

Ironically, the most sophisticated methods of torture were developed by the so-called more civilized societies in Asia and Europe. In Asia, for example, torture was used throughout the ages in China, Japan, and India. In Europe, Rome, Greece, England, and Spain all used it for hundreds of years.

During the earliest years in these countries, torture was most frequently used during the time of war or when a society was engulfed in turmoil. And torture was primarily used as a form of punishment or to terrorize the victim into providing the information desired by the torturer.

One of the most common types of torture that was used from the earliest times and right on through to the eighteenth century in Europe was that of mutilation. L. A. Parry, a scholar, has written that "Eyes and tongues were plucked out, the nose, ears, lips, hands, and feet cut off, the scalp torn away. . . . men without hands, without feet, with the tongue cut out and branded on the forehead . . . could frequently be seen walking about, and were regarded as warnings to others."

As time went on, both ancient Greece and Rome outlawed the use of torture against its citizens. However, that rule did not apply to slaves because they were considered inferior and did not enjoy the same rights as full-fledged citizens.

Thus, in the city-state of Athens, a slave's word was not believed to be the truth unless his or her testimony was given while being tortured. The officials simply did not believe that the slaves would tell the truth unless forced into doing so.

The types of torture that were used in Greece were extremely brutal. For instance, victims were publicly whipped with heavy hogskin whips or burned to death. People were also stretched on the rack, which was a device that literally pulled a person's body apart.

On the other hand, Roman officials usually tried to avoid torturing the slaves. At first they attempted to get the truth by questioning the slave. If that did not work, then torture was used. A judge determined how much torture was to be used. And while the torturers usually had orders not to kill a victim, that advice often went unheeded.

Even though torture was legal under certain conditions in both ancient Greece and Rome, many citizens criticized its use. Some even called on their governments to stop using it. In doing so, these critics claimed that the use of torture made people lie rather than tell the truth. This was because people would often say anything the authorities wanted to hear in order to stop the pain.

Later, during the Middle Ages—the period between ancient and modern times—torture was used much more frequently. It, in fact, became a popular weapon of both the Roman Catholic Church and medieval rulers.

During this period the Church required total loyalty of its followers. Those who disobeyed the Church frequently became victims of the Inquisition. The Inquisition was a tribunal established by the popes in order to repress heresy (not believing in or following the Church's teachings). It primarily took place in France, Germany, Italy, and Spain.

While the Inquisition did torture and imprison people, it rarely sentenced them to death. The worst cases of abuse occurred during the Spanish Inquisition, which was separate from the Papal Inquisition and which was initiated and directed by Spanish rulers for political reasons. During the Spanish Inquisition over 2,000 suspected heretics were tortured to death, and 17,000 more were mutilated.

The Church also used to torture to punish its enemies. Thus, torture was not used purely for religious reasons.

The rulers at this time were basically dictators and demanded that everyone obey them. They felt that the only way they could force people to do that was through the threat of torture. The use of torture was so widespread that special torture chambers were built.

A man is being whipped in the Middle East.

In England, people who were found guilty of crimes like murder or witchcraft were severely punished. The most common punishment was torture on the rack. Sometimes, however, murderers were publicly boiled to death. Also, when a person insulted or even questioned the authority of the government, the person was often publicly whipped, had one or both ears chopped off, his nose slit with a knife, and his forehead branded with a red-hot iron bar. Some prisoners were thrown into dungeons with rats. When the prisoners tried to sleep, the rats would attack and rip flesh from their bodies.

English citizens were more or less saved from these cruelties when the English Bill of Rights was drafted in 1689. It stated that "cruel and unusual punishment ought not be inflicted." From that point on, torture was used less and less in England.

While some people during the Middle Ages cried out against the brutality of torture, real headway to slow its use did not take place until the eighteenth century. That century has been called the period of the "Enlightenment." The word "enlightenment" means "being freed from ignorance." During this century people began questioning the old ways of life and began moving toward a more humanitarian way of living. As a result, torture began to be seen as a barbaric and savage practice.

During this period France issued its famous human rights document, the Declaration of the Rights of Man. That document abolished torture "forever." At the same time, French law made torture a crime equal to murder.

For the first time in history, the right not to be tortured was considered a "natural" human right and not simply a political right. It meant that torture was a violation of the human rights of people regardless of their political or religious beliefs. However, while the French may have halted the use of torture, many other countries continued to use it.

141

The overall human rights situation continued to improve throughout the nineteenth century. For many different reasons—including a move toward a more humanitarian way of life and a shift from an agricultural to an industrial economy—many nations abolished slavery. And as people became more humane, the practice of torture began to be perceived as both primitive and cruel. Thus, many nations also stopped using public whippings, brandings, and other forms of torture.

By the 1920s a scholar declared that torture was a "practice forever left behind in man's journey toward progress." It may have looked that way then, but those of us living today know that just the opposite is true.

Torture in Today's World

Since the late 1930s, the use of torture in the world has continued to increase. This is true despite the fact that there are now many laws, conventions, and agreements that prohibit the use of torture.

During World War II both the Japanese and the Germans tortured civilians and prisoners of war. This was done both to gain information about their enemies and to punish them.

At the same time, during the Holocaust, Nazi Germany set up torture chambers within its death camps. Torturelike "medical experiments" were also conducted on the Jews, Gypsies, and others.

These medical experiments were both bizarre and extremely painful. For example, Jews were placed in freezing water in order to see how long it would take for them to pass out or die. The results of these experiments were later used to design special cold-resistant flight suits for German pilots. Nazi doctors also stuck needles with blue dye into the eyes of those Jews who had one blue and one brown eye. This experiment was conducted to see if the brown eye could be turned into another blue eye. Also, while fully awake, many Jewish twins were cut open and had their hearts, livers, and other vital organs examined and/or taken out. Many of these "experiments" were conducted merely to satisfy the curiosity of certain Nazi doctors.

Most of these human guinea pigs either died on the spot or were later gassed to death. One witness to this torture later said, "The people suffered such horrible pain that I could hardly stand to be near them."

Following World War II, many people in Africa and Asia fought in revolutions in order to gain their freedom. During these battles torture was often used as a weapon by both sides—by the people fighting for their freedom and by those already in power. Terrorists and revolutionaries in other parts of the world have also used torture against their opponents and enemies.

Over the past forty years or more, many governments have used torture for various reasons. As previously stated, in this day and age torture takes place both in democratic countries as well as those under dictatorships.

Why Torture Is Used

While torture sometimes takes place just because a government or military official is mean or angry, this is not the main reason why it is carried out. Rather, in most cases, the use of torture is part of a very detailed and systematic plan developed by the government. Quite often, governments use torture because they think it is effective in accomplishing some of their goals.

One goal is to obtain information or a "confession." If a government fears that its opponents are getting too strong or are going to try to overthrow it, then it may torture a person in order to get information that is crucial to its national security. Such information may include the plans and activities of its enemies.

In other cases, however, a government may be so power—hungry that it makes up any excuse to punish its critics. In this situation a government may falsely accuse its critics of plotting to carry out a revolution. The government then uses this as a "good" excuse to torture and kill them.

A recent case in Brazil presents an example of this situation. Policemen arrested a young man named Marcos Arruda because he was having dinner with a woman who belonged to a political group the government authorities did not trust. Once in jail, the police tortured Marcos in order to force him to provide information about the woman's political group. Since he did not belong to the group and had just met the woman, Marcos really did not have any information to give. But the police did not believe him and kept up the torture.

Of the torture he suffered, Marcos said: "After punching me and clubbing me . . . they began to give me electric shocks . . . and continued to beat me brutally. . . . The electric shocks and the beatings continued for several hours. [They gave] me terrible shocks on my face, in my ears, eyes, mouth and nostrils. One of the policemen remarked, 'Look, he is letting off sparks. Put it in his ear now.' The torture was so serious and long-lasting that I thought I would die. . . . I was swallowing my tongue and could only breathe with difficulty. . . . [Later,] they burnt my shoulder with cigarette stubs; they put the barrel of a revolver into my mouth saying they would kill me."

In that rare event when government officials actually acknowledge that their countries do use torture, many will argue that it is a necessary evil. For instance, one Argentine soldier said, "Nobody wants to be called a torturer. The word stinks of cowardice. But nobody ever gave any important in-

144

formation because a gentleman came up to him and said, 'Please tell me what you know.'" Be that as it may, the use of torture for any reason is widely condemned by most people around the world.

Torture is also often used to break a person down or force one to renounce or give up his or her own religious or political beliefs. As recently as the late 1970s, for example, Jewish political prisoners in Argentina were forced to renounce their religion.

One of these former prisoners reported that "From the moment Jewish people were kidnapped, they were tortured. Some of them were made to kneel in front of pictures of Hitler and Mussolini to renounce their origins."

In a similar but somewhat different vein, some governments use torture to intimidate or frighten people into quitting political activity that the government officials frown

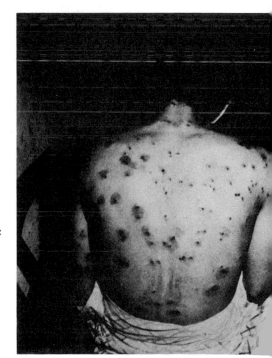

This man was burned with electric shocks and cigarettes.

145

upon. Such officials often figure that if they kill or torture several people then all the others will "get the message." Among the nations that have recently used torture in this way are the following: Guatemala, El Salvador, Chile, Uruguay, Argentina, Brazil, Syria, Turkey, Iran, Afghanistan, South Africa, and the Soviet Union. And that is just a partial list of all the nations that have used and/or continue to use torture in that manner.

An English language teacher in Romania, in Eastern Europe, knows all about how governments use torture to try to frighten their people. Right after he joined the Free Trade Union movement in his country, the top three union leaders were arrested. As a result, the teacher took over the union. Within a month, he was also arrested. During his time in prison, he was repeatedly beaten.

"They started beating us on a table," he has said, "telling us . . . before the beating, 'You are my victim. You will be killed. You won't get out of this building.'"

He was lucky. He did get out of prison alive and then moved to the United States.

As for another example, in the early 1980s, the Guatemalan government used torture and murder to tighten its control over its citizens. In order to discourage people from supporting those who opposed the government, officials tortured thousands of citizens. Many times the tortured bodies were then thrown into the streets, and photographs of their mutilated bodies were printed in the newspapers. All of this was done to frighten the other citizens into obeying the government.

Torture is also frequently used to punish people who have been arrested for both political reasons and criminal offenses. In such cases punishment is frequently used in order to either embarrass a person, teach him or her a lesson, and/or to in-

146

These men had a foot amputated for crimes they committed.

flict pain. The methods of torture used to accomplish such ends are numerous and bizarre.

For instance, several years ago the police in Bihar, India, poked out the eyes of several suspected thiefs. After stabbing the prisoners' eyes with needles, the police poured acid on the wounds.

Numerous African, Asian, and Middle Eastern nations publicly whip prisoners who have been found guilty of crimes like robbery, smuggling, and assault. Also, such nations as Iran, Pakistan, Saudi Arabia, and Mauritania regularly amputate or cut off the fingers or hands of thieves.

The Torture of Children
Nothing, many have claimed, is as unjust as the torture of innocent children. Nevertheless, many nations often use torture against children.

While there are many reasons why children are tortured, there are basically four main ones. First, it is used to punish those children who take part in political activities of which their government disapproves. This could include such activities as marching in protests or even complaining about the type of education one is receiving. Second, torture is used to force children to "confess" to political crimes that the government suspects they may have committed. Third, torture is also used on children as a way of punishing their parents for saying or doing something of which the government did not approve. As torturers know only too well, torturing children in front of their parents is another method of torturing the parents. It causes the parents great mental and emotional anguish to see their children brutalized and to hear them shrieking with pain. Fourth, children are frequently forced to watch their parents being tortured. This, too, causes the children and parents extraordinary grief.

Such abuse takes place in many locations around the world. Sometimes it takes place in Europe, but is far more common in Africa, South America, Central America, the Middle East, and Asia.

The types of torture that children have been subjected to are almost too overwhelming to think about. Nevertheless, if people refuse to think about such incidents, then there may be little or no hope of ever halting them. In light of that, several cases involving the torture of children that have taken place in various parts of the world will be presented here.

In the early 1980s, young political prisoners in Poland were forced to take boiling hot showers, and at least one high-school student was beaten to death. These punishments were meted out because the students had protested some of their government's policies.

During the 1980s, numerous black youths in South Africa have been tortured for protesting against the white government's racist policy of apartheid. Some children have been treated so harshly that they have had mental breakdowns.

The South American nation of Chile is notorious for its attacks against children. Simply because two teenagers— Rodrigo Rojas and Carmen Quintana—were taking photographs of an antigovernment demonstration that was being held on July 2, 1980, they were beaten and then set on fire by a group of soldiers. Both badly burned bodies were then dumped into a ditch. Miraculously, Carmen survived, but Rodrigo did not. Prior to Rodrigo's death, his mother visited him in the hospital and said he was so badly burned that the only part of his body she could touch were the soles of his feet.

In El Salvador, which is located in Central America, children are sometimes arrested and tortured because officials suspect the children are working against the government.

Others have been arrested and tortured in order to spread fear among other citizens, and as a warning to them not to criticize or work against the government.

Robert G. Torricelli, a member of the U.S. House of Representatives, inspected some of the prisons in El Salvador in the spring of 1983. He was greatly upset by what he had witnessed: "I saw 13-year-old prisoners who had never been to trial. . . . Some had acid scars from being tortured."

In the Middle Eastern country of Iran, children are both tortured and forced to watch as their parents are tortured. Amnesty International reports that "One mother screamed she was ready to confess [to a crime she did not commit] when she could no longer stand the agony of her 3-year-old daughter being made to watch."

One witness told Amnesty International that "Often the Iranian guards slap the children at the same time [the mother is lashed]. . . . Anyone who has seen the terror of such children cannot easily forget it."

From 1986 to the present hundreds of students in South Korea have been tortured for protesting the lack of freedom in their country. They have been beaten with fists and clubs, shocked with cattle prods, nearly drowned, and threatened with secret executions.

Hundreds of other stories could be told about the torture of children in many other nations around the world, but those that have been told are similar in detail to the others.

Arguments Used for and Against Torture

Different people in different nations have different views about the use of torture. This is not at all surprising because there are often many different points of view concerning any complex issue in life.

Listed below are some of the reasons cited in favor of using torture as well as those used to argue against its use:

For: Sometimes authorities need to torture those terrorists or guerrillas who "have put innocent lives at risk and who endanger both society and the state itself." This could result in the gain of important information that could help make the society a safer place. In some cases, it could also possibly save the lives of hundreds, and possibly thousands, of people.

Against: It is never right to torture a person. Torture is barbaric and inhumane. Besides, the majority of those tortured usually do not have the sort of information the authorities are seeking. Thus, "they are tortured either to force [false] confessions from them" or as a frightening warning not to oppose the government.

For: Torture is the quickest and most efficient way to get information from a suspected terrorist or enemy of the country.

Against: Even if that is sometimes true, torture is still not permissible. It robs a person of his or her human dignity. Furthermore, once torture is used and is seen as an efficient way of obtaining information, authorities too often become reliant on it. As they do so, they tend to use it in place of other, more humane ways to gather information.

For: In many cases torture is the only sure way to get the truth out of someone.

Against: That is not true. Once a person is brutally treated, he or she is very likely to do or say anything. And that includes giving false or fabricated information. That is simply because he or she wishes to stop the torturous pain. Finally, when a person is under great physical and psychological stress, he or she may "suffer hallucinations that distort the truth, even to themselves."

151

For: In an exceptional situation, it is entirely proper to use torture "just once." For instance, it would be permissible to torture a terrorist in order to force him to reveal where he planted a bomb in a city. There is a good chance if he is not tortured that he will not give up the information that could prevent a tragedy from taking place.

Against: If authorities use torture once and it "works," then it is very easy to get "addicted" to its use. Next time torture may be used in another "exceptional case," and then another and another. Before long, authorities may use torture for many different reasons. By then, torture has become an accepted, and not an "exceptional," practice.

For: The use of torture is a proper punishment for people who have committed especially bad crimes. They have made others suffer, and so they should suffer, too.

Against: Punishment must certainly be meted out to those who commit crimes. However, the very idea of justice means that the punishment suffered by a criminal must be fair, and not cruel and barbaric. Since torture is widely believed to be a cruel and unusual punishment, it cannot ever be used in a just manner. Thus, its use does not serve justice. In fact, its use is one of the greatest injustices that can be imagined. And one must keep in mind that "two wrongs do not make a right."

Prevention of Torture

Not a single nation in the world has a clause in its constitution or code of laws that states that torture is legal. Furthermore, the constitutions and laws of at least one hundred twelve nations explicitly prohibit the use of torture. Quite obviously, then, some nations give only lip service to the idea that torture is unjust and inhumane.

As previously noted, there are numerous international treaties, declarations, and conventions that outlaw the use of torture by anyone for any reason. In addition to Article 5 of the Universal Declaration of Human Rights, the Geneva Convention (one of a series of agreements concerning the treatment of prisoners of war) also forbids the practice of torture, stating that "outrages upon personal dignity, in particular, humiliating and degrading treatment" are forbidden. Also, Article 7 of the International Covenant on Civil and Political Rights states that "No one shall be subjected to torture or to cruel, inhuman or degrading treatment or punishment. In particular, no one shall be subjected without his free consent to medical or scientific experimentation."

In 1975, the United Nations adopted the Declaration on the Protection of All Persons from Torture and Other Cruel, Inhuman or Degrading Treatment or Punishment. Agreed upon by all 144 of the nations that were members of the UN in 1975, the declaration states, in part, that "Exceptional circumstances such as a state of war or a threat of war, internal political instability or other public emergency may not be invoked as a justification of torture or other cruel, inhuman or degrading treatment or punishment." The declaration was a first step toward ending torture, but it did not carry any legal force to punish those who committed torture.

Then in 1984 the United Nations General Assembly adopted the UN Convention Against Torture. This convention adds legal force to the declaration. Those nations that "ratify the convention must make torture a criminal offense under the laws of their country." They also must agree to allow the torturers to be prosecuted wherever they are caught. That means that a torturer cannot escape to another country and expect to go free. In addition to stating that "torture can never be justified," the convention also states that a torturer's plea of innocence by claiming that he or she was simply following orders will not be considered a valid excuse. As a result, each and every person has to take responsibility for his or her own actions.

The convention is potentially a major step in preventing future cases of torture. However, far fewer than half of the United Nations member states have even signed the convention, let alone ratified it.

Both the problem of ratifying the convention as well as the fact that torture is still widely used by many nations around the world raises the question, "Can anything really be done to prevent torture from taking place?" The answer is "Yes, something can and is being done."

One classic example of what is being done to try to halt torture is the work of Amnesty International's Urgent Action Network. The network is on call twenty-four hours a day, and its main purpose is to try to save people from being tortured or executed.

Scott Harrison, a U.S. citizen and the network director for Amnesty International USA, explains how the network works: "We have the names of victims and potential victims, and we tell officials, prison doctors, and others that we're watching closely. We also send copies of our letters and telegrams to their superiors. We keep going back to the same authorities with the same requests to tell us why they're holding someone . . . and to make sure that torture isn't being used. So we not only help individual victims, but also let authorities know that we'll always be there watching. We'll be right around the corner every day, week after week . . . Our position is clear: No one should be tortured."

Over fifty thousand people in over ninety countries are members of the Urgent Action Network. When contacted about a person who is in danger of being tortured, members immediately send off letters to the officials of the government who are threatening to torture the person. The letters inform the authorities that people around the world care about the potential victim and remind them that torture is inhumane, immoral, and illegal.

But one may ask, "Is the Urgent Action Network really putting a stop to torture?" Harrison is quite sure that it is. "We are effective in stopping some individual cases of torture," he says, "and in signaling government authorities that we can launch massive efforts if they violate human rights. And our work constantly gets better, more sophisticated, more effective."

Many other local and national organizations—like church groups, trade unions, minority rights groups, members of political parties—around the world are also working to prevent torture from taking place. To accomplish their goals they conduct antitorture campaigns, hold protests, go to court, issue public appeals, inspect prisons and visit prisoners, petition governments, and provide information both to the press as well as to nongovernmental human rights organizations like Amnesty International.

Sometimes such actions actually do prevent the use of torture. Torture in Brazil was largely stopped in the 1970s after that nation's powerful Catholic Church put heavy pressure on the military government to halt its inhumane actions. Also, in 1979, the British government stanched the use of torture against prisoners in Ireland following a forceful outcry from both the public and police surgeons.

But in many other situations torture continues to take place. Because of that, human rights activists across the globe are not satisfied with what they have accomplished thus far, and continue to work and speak out against torture. They know, as Amnesty International has pointed out, that "silence, more than any instrument to inflict pain on another human being, is essential to the business of torture."

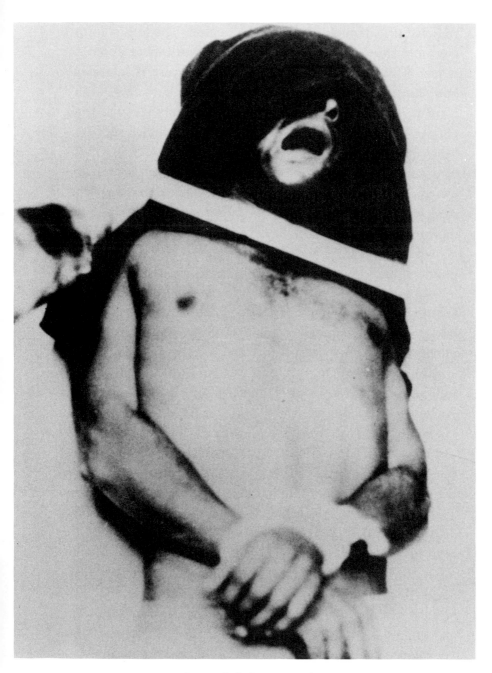

A man is being tortured.

Prosecuting Torturers

Most torturers in most nations have never been punished for the crimes they have committed. That is primarily true because their actions have either been condoned or ignored by their governments.

But as of late, a small number of countries have begun to prosecute torturers. This is due to many factors, including the recent international outcry against torture, and a call by both torture victims and human rights groups that justice be carried out against torturers. Spain, England, and Greece are among the nations that have recently prosecuted them.

During the mid-1980s the government of Argentina also began to imprison the numerous torturers who were responsible for torturing thousands of people throughout the late 1970s and early 1980s. But then the government suddenly refused to continue the prosecutions. In fact, in 1986 it passed a law with the intent of "largely halting the prosecutions of Argentine military officers accused of human rights violations." Why did that happen? First, military leaders warned that if the prosecutions continued there was a good chance that their troops (many of whom had committed torture) may rise up against the government. The government leaders also felt that the ongoing trials were causing more grief and division in the country than they were worth. Former torture victims and human rights activists, however, disagreed and called for the continuation of the trials. They claimed that if the torturers were not punished then it would send out a message that torturers can get away with their illegal actions. It seems as if this is going to be a very controversial issue for a long time to come in Argentina.

Other nations are also refusing to punish those who have tortured others. Brazil and Uruguay provide clear examples of such nations.

Between 1969 and 1973 thousands of Brazilians were tortured by over four hundred Brazilian torturers. It is reported that these torturers used at least two hundred thirty-eight different types of torture on their victims. However, because of the lack of commitment on the Brazilian government's part, it appears doubtful that any of the torturers will ever be brought to trial.

Throughout most of the 1970s and the early part of the 1980s many citizens of Uruguay were tortured because of their political beliefs. But, like Argentina, Uruguay has passed a law that gives "a full amnesty for human rights violations committed during military rule from 1973 to 1985."

Situations such as these force one to wonder, "Can torture, once and for all, be stopped?" That is a question that is now being seriously debated and examined by many governments, the United Nations, and numerous human rights groups around the world.

Ending Torture
Some human rights experts claim that torture can be halted once and for all. Others say that they doubt it can. They have these doubts because they believe that some humans, in certain circumstances, will always have a tendency to mistreat those who are less powerful than themselves.

Those who assert that torture can be stopped admit that it will not be easy to accomplish. However, they point out that the abolition of slavery did not come about easily either. Nevertheless, today the institution of slavery is universally condemned and a rare occurrence in our world.

The leaders of Amnesty International, who believe that torture can be halted, state that "what is currently lacking is the political will of governments to stop torturing people. It is as simple as that and as difficult as that."

Given this belief, human rights groups plan to continue to work for the ratification of the United Nations Convention Against Torture and Other Cruel, Inhumane or Degrading Treatment or Punishment. Then, and only then, they believe will there be a hope that the act of torture will become as rare as the institution of slavery.

"We spend more money on dog food than we do on the 600 million people in the world who are malnourished."

—John Gilligan, former administrator, Agency for International Development

7

Hunger

Within one minute after you have begun reading this sentence, twenty-five men, women, and children, mostly children, will have died from hunger. In the next hour, the death toll will be about fifteen hundred. Within 24 hours, over thirty-five thousand will have starved to death. The pain and death of hunger can be seen throughout the world, on the streets of Calcutta, India, in the homes of Harlem in New York, and in the deserts of Ethiopia.

The scene is a relief center in Ethiopia. Hundreds of starving children, women, and men stand, sit, or lie on the barren, desert ground waiting to be treated by a handful of nurses and one doctor. The hospital is a round, large, brown, canvas tent. There is a constant wind knocking against the canvas. Dust is blowing everywhere both inside the tent and outside. Here there are children, many children. They are dying of starvation and diseases related to the lack of proper food. Their lives tell a common story—a short story from life to death. One such child, whom we shall call Miriam Mustafah, is fourteen.

As you look at Miriam, the first thing you notice is how large a head she seems to have. Actually, her head is not all that large. But compared to the skinny, bony body, and her very narrow neck, her head seems strangely large. There are other features you notice about Miriam. Her rib cage seems glued to a matchstick body, and her stomach sticks out, swollen and round. As she stares at you, you are almost embarrassed to look her in the eye. Miriam's eyes seem large and round; they appear to bulge out somehow as she stares aimlessly in your direction. Miriam and many children like her are dying—dying because they do not have sufficient food; they are dying of hunger.

Of the more than thirty-five thousand people who die each day of hunger or a disease brought on by hunger, about twenty-five thousand are children under the age of five. The most basic of all human rights is the right to live. Those who suffer from hunger are denied that right.

But just what is hunger? What are hunger-related diseases? Why are so many innocent people dying of hunger? And what can be done to stop this silent killer of children, women, and men?

Hunger, Illness, and Disease
Hunger is the pain or weakness one has when he or she lacks enough food over a period of time. Chronic hunger is hunger over a long period of time, days, months, even years. Persons suffering from chronic hunger never receive enough food. Their bodies lose weight and become so weak that they can do very little. Chronic hunger also affects the mind. One's ability to think and concentrate is reduced. These effects of hunger are experienced by an American farmer, Moritz Thomsen, in Senator Ernest Hollings' book *The Case Against Hunger.*

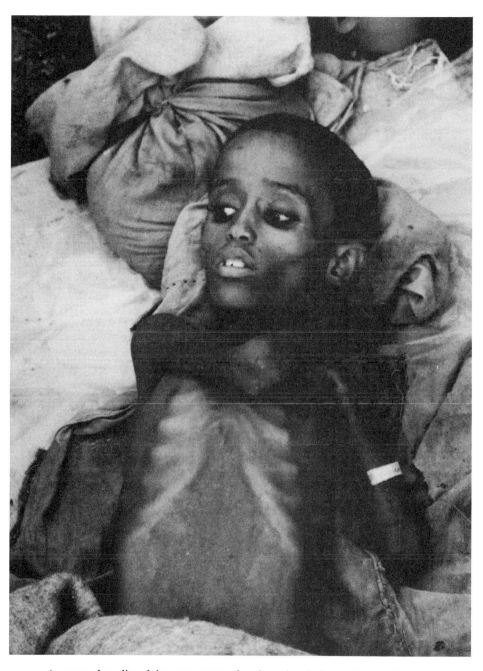

A young boy lies dying at a camp for drought victims in Bati, Ethiopia.

Thomsen had joined the Peace Corps. The Peace Corps is a volunteer organization sponsored by the U.S. government. Americans who volunteer for the Peace Corps are sent various places throughout the world to help people improve their lives and standards of living. Thomsen was sent to a village in rural Ecuador (in South America) where his job was to help people improve their raising of food. Food was so scarce in the village that he began to suffer from hunger along with others living there. Thomsen described his experience with hunger and its effects.

> It was bananas that saved my life. . . . Trying to set an example, I was clearing land on a daily schedule, and it became a fascinating problem . . . to stuff the bananas into myself and see how far I could go. Two bananas would fill me up for forty minutes or fifty minutes of low-keyed work. One banana would get me down the hill. Sixteen bananas would see me through until noon if I didn't work too fast. . . . It was also a growing mental depression, a gray fog of hopelessness that grew in my head each day. I could feel myself getting stupider. Things became . . . irritating to me.

People suffering from hunger are more likely to become ill since their bodies cannot fight off illness and disease. What would normally be a minor or short-term illness for one not suffering from hunger could mean death for the victim of hunger. In Phnom Penh, Kampuchea, former *New York Times* reporter Sydney Schanberg saw children suffering from diseases caused by hunger and reported that "Some have swollen bellies. Some are shrunken. A 10-year-old girl has dehydrated to the size of a 4-year-old. Harsh . . . coughs come from their throats, marking the beginnings of pneumonia and tuberculosis. All have dysentery. . . . Their skins have turned scaly."

164

Malnutrition. Malnutrition describes what happens to the body when a person is not receiving the right kinds and amounts of food needed to keep the body healthy. When there is a variety of foods that provide all the building blocks for a healthy body but not enough of one or more of these foods, then a condition called undernutrition occurs. Malnutrition and undernutrition seem to go hand in hand.

Malnutrition may lead to illnesses that cause permanent damage or death. This is especially true among children where physical and mental damage is often permanent. Vitamins, proteins, carbohydrates (starches and sugars), fats, and minerals are body-building materials. A proper balance of these materials is necessary for a healthy mind and body. They are found in green or yellow vegetables, citrus, fruits, legumes, milk products, fish, and meat. An improper balance of these building materials or an insufficient amount of one or more may cause a number of health problems. While working in India, W. Stanley Mooneyham came across a family in the village of Siuli Bari.

> Adary Mal hunched over the little pot where the family's one meal for the day was cooking. Bubbling in the pot was a wad of weeds. One of her six children squatted beside her, picking through a handful of snails gathered from the fields that day. This would be the only protein they would have.

Such a limited diet may cause gum disease and loss of teeth, growth stunting, scurvy, blindness, rickets, body sores, a bulging stomach, and brain damage. Unhealthy diets are found in the United States as well. Poor people often suffer from malnutrition because they do not have enough money to purchase necessary foods.

165

In his book, *Poverty in America,* Milton Meltzer describes an American Hispanic family who lived in a one-room shack. Not having enough money, they ate only tortillas and beans. This is all they had for breakfast, lunch, and supper. Although tortillas and beans contain all of the necessary proteins needed in a diet, other building blocks for a healthy body are lacking. The children were also always hungry. They were more likely to become ill than children with a proper diet. Meltzer also interviewed a doctor who treated poor Hispanic farm workers in Texas. The doctor explained:

> The majority of my patients wander all over America working the crops. . . . They are hungry. Our people have become human garbage. . . . I am told that elephants don't die of disease; they die of starvation when their teeth fall out. That is the same thing that happens to my patients.

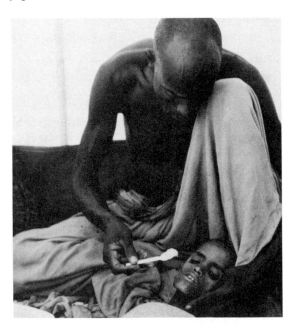

A father feeds his dying son who is suffering from severe malnutrition in Southern Africa.

When people maintain a limited diet without a proper balance of protein or not enough protein a disease known as kwashiorkor may occur. Kwashiorkor is most noticeable among children. Their growth is stunted, sores develop on the skin, and the body swells. In Mexico, kwashiorkor was called the snakeskin because a child's skin would peel off. The lack of protein may also cause brain damage in young children under the age of five. When people do not receive enough protein, they do not have much energy and seem not to care about very much. "Many visitors to poor villages might think that the people are lazy and do not want to improve their lot. But they do not understand the influence of diet on the ability and health of these villagers," explained a doctor from Mexico.

Having explored the meaning of hunger and some of the problems it causes, one might ask why there is hunger. Is it simply a matter of not enough food to feed everyone? Is hunger an inescapable part of life; a roll of the dice—if you end up in a plentiful country you live; a poor producing country, you die? Or is there more to it than meets the eye? Let us now explore the causes of hunger.

Causes of Hunger
When food is very scarce and people in a particular place are faced with the problem of starving to death, we refer to this lack of enough food as a famine. Famine or the scarcity of food may be due to natural or human causes. In order to understand why people are starving and dying of hunger and hunger-related diseases, we shall explore famine and its causes.

Natural Causes of Famine and Hunger. Natural causes of famine and hunger have existed for thousands of years. One of the major natural causes of famine is the lack of rainfall.

Drought or the lack of rainfall over a long period of time results in the loss of crops. It also prevents the growth of vegetation that provides food for livestock such as cattle, sheep, and pigs. When people are dependent upon such crops and livestock, they are in for hard times as the ground becomes barren and animals die for want of water and grazing fields. Eventually, people also die. In the African countries of Niger and Mali, writer Claire Sterling reported that during a famine, cattle raisers could be found "sitting near where their cattle had perished, . . . [they said] they were waiting for death themselves."

Cases of drought-related famines have been recorded throughout time. In the Bible, we find the story of Jacob and his family who moved from Canaan to Egypt because of a famine in the land due to the lack of rain. While in Egypt, the biblical story relates how Joseph, Jacob's son, was placed in charge of storing grain for an expected drought famine which lasted for seven years. Whether or not one believes the details of these biblical stories is a personal matter. What is of interest to us is that famine was a major concern of ancient peoples.

Famines are mentioned throughout the historical writings of India. In his book, *The History and Economics of Indian Famines,* British historian A. Loveday presents an ancient Indian account of the famine between 917 and 918:

> One could scarcely see the water in the Vitasta [river] . . . entirely covered as the river was with corpses soaked and swollen by the water in which they had long been lying. The land became densely covered with bones in all directions, until it was like one great burial-ground, causing terror to all beings.

In ancient Rome, drought brought about a famine in 450 B.C. By 436 B.C., it seemed to many that the famine would

168

never end. In despair, thousands of Romans committed suicide by throwing themselves into the Tiber River. In more recent history, millions of people have perished due to famines.

During the famine of 1769 and 1770 in northeastern India, it is estimated that ten million people died from hunger. This is more than the population of any major cities in the United States: New York, Chicago, or Los Angeles. About a hundred years later, another famine caused by drought occurred in China. This famine claimed the lives of over nine million persons. During this Chinese famine, organized mobs did whatever they could to find money so as to buy food. They robbed stores and homes. Clothing was stolen from corpses and sold in the marketplace. Men sold their wives and children. Children suffering from hunger were killed by their own parents, who then committed suicide. As the famine worsened, people began to eat the remains of dead people. Then they began killing and eating fellow human beings. In marketplaces, human meat was sold for food.

Drought struck in Africa during the late 1960s and lasted until 1974. As the drought tightened its grip over these areas, people watched as their herds and other animals died. A Nigerian woman reflected on this slow painful experience.

> Last year it was the animals, we could do nothing as we watched them die, watched them withering away until they would just stop and sit down with no strength to fight any longer. But for some reason there was hope while they lived. We knew that after they were gone we were next. Last year it was the animals. This year it is us.

And when the next year came, it brought starvation and death to thousands. Other African nations south of the Sahara Desert were also affected. Colin Morris, a British missionary living in Zambia, tells of a man dropping dead "not a hundred yards from my front door." The doctors found a few leaves and a ball of grass in the man's stomach.

In the 1980s, Africans suffered another drought. This drought brought millions of people to the brink of starvation. Almost 45 percent of the total area of Africa was affected. That is 5,265,000 square miles or almost one and a half times greater than the entire area of the United States. The drought spread devastation over Mali, Niger, Chad, Sudan, Ethiopia, Somalia, Kenya, Uganda, Tanzania, and Mozambique.

Even as rains fell in 1985, the damage of this drought could not be overcome immediately. During the dry years from 1980 to 1985, the United Nations Food and Agriculture Organization estimated that five billion tons of top soil needed to grow food and other vegetation had been blown away or eroded. In this case, the erosion occurred when plant life died, and there were no roots to hold the soil in place. By 1985, it was reported that three out of four of those people living in drought-stricken Africa had neither enough food nor shelter to maintain their health. Over 150 million people in this area were near starvation.

In Ethiopia, 3,000 people were dying each day due to hunger and related diseases. Miles Harris, a doctor working in Ethiopia, described his experiences in his book *Breakfast in Hell.* He painfully tells of trying to save a starving child by forcing liquid into the child's mouth. The boy could not take it: ". . . there was movement of the jaw, half way between a yawn and bite, and then the face relaxed." The father leaned forward and closed the eyes of the dead child. In Mozambique, 100,000 people starved to death during 1984.

Throughout the land, people drifted aimlessly across borders in search of help. Approximately a million people left Ethiopia for Sudan. Another 400,000 entered from Chad, and 250,000 came from Uganda. At the same time, a half million

Sudanese had been forced to leave their homes in search of relief from the drought. They sought shelter and food. Many, especially children, were almost naked. As they died, their delicate sticklike bodies quickly decayed upon the barren ground, for there was so little left of them.

Other natural causes for famine and hunger may be due to diseases that kill off livestock. In bodies of water, poisonous algae kill thousands of fish which people in an area depend upon for food. Hurricanes, tornadoes, freezing weather, earthquakes, and floods have been known to destroy both crops and livestock. On May 24, 1985, a typhoon struck

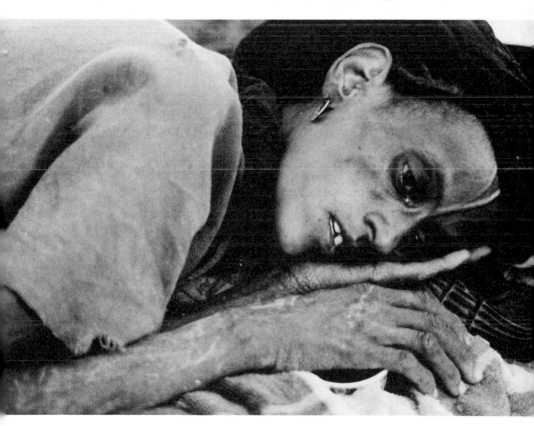

A drought victim lies unconscious awaiting medical treatment in Africa.

Bangladesh, a country on the northeast border of India. In addition to causing thousands of deaths, many more people lost their homes and food. A long-term problem was the loss of crops and the need for seeds for the next planting. Without assistance from other nations, Bangladesh faced increased hunger and famine due to this natural disaster.

In 1983, unfavorable weather conditions caused a 50 percent drop in corn production in the United States. Although this did not cause a famine in the United States, it influenced the distribution of food to peoples in other countries where food is in short supply and in famine-stricken areas. This is important when we consider that the United States supplies 75 percent of all corn to the rest of the world and that corn is used to feed both animals and people.

Pests, such as locusts, are another cause of famine. They can destroy an entire community's crops in a matter of hours. In Nigeria at the end of the 1800s, the people of Bauchi were threatened with starvation after a swarm of locusts destroyed most of the food crops.

Bunt and smut, fungus diseases, are known to attack grass, corn, and cereals such as wheat. In America, the loss of corn from smut has been more than fifty million bushels in one year alone. Between 1846 and 1847, disease destroyed most of the potato crop in Ireland. One person who suffered through this famine stated that "It didn't matter who was related to you, your friend was whoever would give you a bite to put in your mouth. . . . The famine killed everything." This famine led to a major immigration of Irish people to the United States. Nevertheless, over one million people died as a result of the failure of the potato crop in Ireland.

Although many famines are closely related to natural conditions and events, they are often the results of drought and improper use of the land by people. Some land is not good for

172

farming, while other land is not good for grazing. Overgrazed land often suffers from erosion during a time of drought because there is little vegetation to hold the topsoil. In farming, when the same crops are planted year after year, the mineral content of the soil decreases and fewer and weaker crops are grown.

Many of these problems might be avoided by proper crop rotation, restricted animal grazing, and selected planting of crops suited to particular areas.

Human Causes of Famine and Hunger. While natural causes of famine and hunger take a heavy toll in lives, the problem is increased by human acts. In fact, it has been suggested that natural famines can be prevented throughout the world. However, the desire for wealth and power appears to have added to the causes of famine and hunger. We may well ask ourselves whether or not world hunger can be reduced if people will cooperate—rid themselves of petty rivalries and jealousies—and limit their desire for wealth and power. However, this may be much easier said than done.

From time immemorial people have competed for wealth and power. Nations and their leaders have sought to spread their influence to achieve two goals. The first goal of all nations is to survive, to have enough food, shelter, and clothing for their people. This first or primary goal also includes the ability to be safe from outside interference—to have physical security. The second goal is to gain more wealth and power than is necessary for their survival and security. This, of course, provides greater luxuries and conveniences. Some nations are so poor and weak that achieving their primary goals is a daily struggle.

These poorer countries have been called lesser developed or underdeveloped nations. Powerful and wealthy nations are called developed nations. These more developed nations are often involved in seeking greater power and wealth than is needed to survive. What may seem odd is that we can find hunger and its effects in both lesser developed and developed nations.

In very poor countries where famines exist, these causes merely add to the problem. The ownership and unfair distribution of land have increased the problem of hunger in these countries. The situation in Bangladesh illustrates this problem.

Bangladesh is a lesser developed nation. It has a population of approximately one hundred million people. The average person takes in 1,800 calories per day, which is about 85 percent of the minimum amount recommended by health agencies. Nevertheless, 96 percent of these calories are in the form of rice, bananas, mangoes, and sweet potatoes. Since these foods are insufficient in protein and other nutrients and eaten in insufficient amounts, the people are undernourished. Sixty percent of the people suffer from a lack of protein. One out of every four children dies before the age of five. The people of Bangladesh have a life expectancy of about eighteen years compared to over seventy years for Americans.

Of the land used for agriculture in Bangladesh, more than 90 percent is owned by only one out of every ten farm families. Six out of ten farm families own only 10 percent of the agricultural land. The remaining families who make their living from agriculture do not own land. They must rent land and share what is produced with the owner. Or, they may work the owner's land for a set wage.

In this case, the hired hand usually receives enough pay to enable him or her to work the next day. After the planting or harvesting season, these laborers find themselves unemployed until the next season. During the off-season, unemployed workers are faced with possible starvation. One such worker,

Hussain Amad, has said that, "When we have no work, there is no food, nothing for my wife and children. Sometimes we beg in the city. Finding food thrown out. But it is not safe. People fight and grab what they can get."

The renting farmer or sharecropper, as he is called, usually receives either half or one third of the amount produced. The landowner receives the remaining half or two thirds. In order to understand the problem, let us consider the case of a landowner who rents out one hundred parcels of land to ten sharecroppers with the understanding that what is produced will be shared fifty-fifty.

Each sharecropper has one parcel. If each parcel of land produces 100 bushels of rice, a total of 1,000 bushels will be produced from among all the sharecroppers. The landowner will receive 50 bushels from each sharecropper or a total of 500 bushels of rice. On the other hand, since each sharecropper produced only 100 bushels, then each will receive 50 bushels of rice. The profit made by the landowner can be used to buy more land and other luxuries. He may continue to get wealthier.

In the meantime, the sharecropper must use his share to feed himself and his family. He must also pay for the seed and fertilizer used in planting and raising the crop. Because his income barely covers basic expenses, he will never be able to save. In fact, he is constantly in debt. In their book, *Needless Hunger,* Betsy Hartmann and James Boyce relate the story of Sharifa. Sharifa once owned land, but is now a sharecropper. "No matter how hard we worked, . . . we never had enough money. We started selling things—our wooden bed, our cattle, our plow, our wedding gifts. Finally, we began to sell the land." Chances are that Sharifa, his wife, and others like them will remain poor with no hope of improvement.

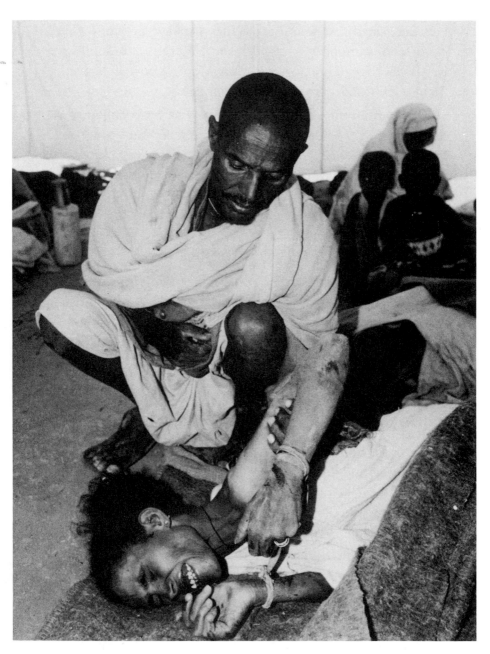

A husband watches over his severely malnourished wife as she lies in agony at a camp for drought victims in Ethiopia.

This illustration is not limited to Bangladesh. The problem of wealth in the hands of a few at the expense of the many is found throughout much of the world. In Java, the major island of Indonesia, one in a hundred landowners controls one third of all farmland. In India, 8 percent of the farming families own more than half of the land that can be used for agriculture. Similar cases can be found in Latin America such as in Colombia where 1 percent of the farmers own over one thousand acres and 99 percent own less than seven acres.

In many of these countries, the poor are often near starvation while the few benefit. It is this type of situation that makes the poor resent their lot. Revolutionaries often appeal to the poor landowners, sharecroppers, landless wage earners, and those who view this type of condition as unfair. They promise to divide the land equally among the poor. However, even after a revolution, the problems of hunger and poverty often remain, for several different reasons.

First, a political revolution may be accompanied by technological changes that take time to accomplish. Second, the amount of land and resources available may be insufficient to support the population. So redistribution of the land may not be a cure-all. Third, new leaders and their friends may take the best sources of wealth, including land for themselves.

International Companies. Another cause for continued hunger in lesser developed countries is the misuse of the land by big international companies and greedy political leaders. These companies usually strike a deal with the government's leaders and are permitted to set up an agricultural business in the country or to work through a local company. Sometimes the foreign business will take out a large loan from the country's national bank. Since the country is poor to begin with, the loan may be large enough to prevent local persons from getting loans to improve their businesses. In Brazil, one fourth of all land that is suitable for agriculture belongs to international companies. This land is used to produce soybeans which are exported to other nations.

Usually, the foreign company purchases large amounts of land for cultivation. The former small landowners, sharecroppers, and wage workers are employed by the international companies to work the land, but what the laborers produce does not support them adequately. What is produced is exported to other nations and provides a large profit for the companies. This means that food and clothing must be imported from other countries. Food and clothing imported from the outside costs more than if it had been locally produced. Therefore, the laborers must use what little they earn for these more expensive imports. They save little or nothing.

In Guatemala, a large American-owned company, known for its canned fruits and vegetables, purchased 57,000 acres of land. Only 9,000 acres are used. The remaining land is left unproductive. At one time, this land was worked by small farmers. Now, many farmers are at the mercy of the large company. With less land available to work, the farmers find it necesary to take lower pay to get hired by the company. In turn, the company is able to have a ready work force at the cheapest possible cost. The food produced is sent to the United States and other more developed countries where a greater profit can be made from the sale of the produce.

While lesser developing countries are producing more food, the people in these countries are eating less of what they produce. Beef production in Costa Rica increased by four times over the past twenty years, yet the amount of beef eaten by Costa Ricans has dropped almost 50 percent. Fish is a major export in the Philippines, Thailand, and Malaysia. Large companies have increased their exports of fish while the people in these countries are eating less fish.

For instance, while the Philippines has increased general food production by 50 percent, three fourths of Filipino children under the age of five are not receiving enough food. This might be partly explained by the fact that only a small amount of what foreign companies produce is sold to the people in that country. For example, Dole and Del Monte, two U.S.-based companies, export 90 percent of what they produce, and only 10 percent of their produce is sold to the Filipinos. Much of this locally sold produce would not be permitted into the United States because it does not meet health standards of the U.S. government.

In Central America, bananas are a major crop for export by large international companies. One such company, United Brands, is involved in the production of pineapple, sugar, vegetable oils, and tea. The company also raises cattle. These products are exported to other developing countries as well as developed countries where they can be sold for a greater profit. In the meanwhile, citizens in these countries that provide such profits are often underfed.

In Peru, where thousands of people go to bed hungry, more fish meal is produced than in any other country. Although fish meal, which is very high in protein, can be used to feed people, it is sent to the United States to feed millions of cats and dogs. In Colombia, flowers are grown for export instead of food crops because it is more profitable to export flowers than to raise food for sale at home. Food must be imported, and imported food costs more than locally grown food. While the exportation of fish meal, bananas, and flowers may be profitable for international companies, it does little to help reduce hunger in these areas.

Hunger and Politics. Sometimes hunger is forced on people because of war, racist policies, and politics. During World War II, Nazi Germany starved millions of Jews and others who were viewed as enemies or subhumans. The Japanese starved prisoners of war during this same period. American and other Allied prisoners suffered from malnutrition and starvation during the wars in Korea and Vietnam. The use of starvation as a military weapon has been used against whole nations. The basic strategy was to cut off supplies of food to the enemy nation and to starve its people into surrendering. A recent example of this was in Nigeria where many thousands of Ibo of Biafra were starved during the civil war of 1967 to 1970.

More recently, war has added to the hunger of many Ethiopians where a civil war has been waging for some time. Antigovernment forces are popular in the northern province of Eritrea. Although enough food was sent to Ethiopia to feed those people who were suffering from the famine during the first half of the 1980s, the Ethiopian government refused to provide relief to those people located in or near Eritrea. This decision was made in order to force people to move south where there is greater support for the government.

In addition, the Ethiopian army took tents, blankets, and clothing, which were meant to aid famine victims, for their own use. In an article in *Life* magazine in 1985, Cheryl McCall reported that in a relief camp in Korem, 15,000 people were fed rations sent for only 6,000. The lack of rations at another camp caused a relief worker to sigh, "It is very frightening when you must decide who will live and who will die, a mother or a child, I pray a lot and cry inside. We are not God. Just helpers."

In many cases, food and equipment sent to famine victims in various countries never reach those people. Some food and other basic needs are stored, because there are not enough trucks to ship the food to outlying areas. During 1985, the African country of Chad needed about fourteen thousand

180

tons of grain per month to feed its starving or underfed population. Nevertheless, with only forty trucks, Chad could distribute very little of what was needed. In addition, there was a shortage of warehouses to store unshipped food that might spoil or be stolen if left outside.

Throughout history, more powerful nations have expanded their power in order to create greater wealth. This expansion of power included the development of colonies. Great Britain, France, Spain, Italy, Portugal, Holland, and Germany have all had their period of colonialism. Colonies were established in Africa, Asia, North America, Latin America, and elsewhere.

Food is being distributed to people in Ethiopia.

The colonies were encouraged to raise cash crops. This permitted the mother country to obtain these crops at a cheaper price than if they were imported from foreign lands. Furthermore, they could be exported and sold at a good profit to still other countries. Investors and owners of plantations could then spend their profits on goods produced in the mother country. All of this benefited the mother country.

Plantations were established to produce coffee, rubber, tobacco, cotton, tea, jute, and other items that had little use in feeding the many poor or small landowners in the colonies. Usually, the colonies developed one or two major cash crops. The raising of other crops was discouraged. This limited the raising of a variety of basic food crops that people in the colonies could use for food. Today, the cash crops of colonial times are still produced by international companies at the expense of the majority of the people in now independent states that were formerly colonies.

The human causes of hunger go hand in hand with natural causes. It has been argued that if natural causes of hunger were our only problem, then we could solve it rather quickly. For example, according to one authority on hunger, if only 10 percent of the food produced in famine-stricken African states were redistributed, there would be no starvation in that area of the world. Yes, there is enough food to feed all of the people on earth. Nevertheless, people are often their own enemy. They often see the world with themselves in the center. As a result, many of those who have seem to want more while those who lack even the basic means for survival die silently.

Hunger in America

The child on the table is eight weeks old and is near death. . . . diarrhea, dehydration, and malnutrition have combined to sap his body weight to two pounds less than his birthweight. The infant is too weak to cry. The child is not in Biafra. He is not in India or Southeast Asia. He is an American. . . .

This was the scene which Senator Ernest F. Hollings found in Mississippi and later described in his book, *The Case Against Hunger*. One might think that it cannot be true. After all, Americans are among the most healthy and well-fed people in the world. Food is so abundant that each day Americans, including families, supermarkets, restaurants, and institutions throw as much as two hundred thousand tons of unused edible food into the garbage. That is a lot of food when one compares it to the fact that Chad needs less than two thousand tons of grain a day to feed its starving population.

Although so much food is thrown out in America each day, thousands of Americans are underfed and under-nourished. In the East Harlem section of New York City, more than four thousand people were faced with the lack of food in 1984. Those with families were asked what they did in order to stay alive. Some said they had to borrow or beg. Others said that they found it necessary to steal in order to get enough food to feed their families.

Hunger exists among all ethnic and racial groups in America. However, it is more common among racial and ethnic minorities. These include blacks, Native Americans, and Hispanics or Spanish-speaking Americans. The reason for this is that large percentages of these people are poor, unemployed, and if employed, hold seasonal and other low-paying jobs. One out of every five American children belong to a poor family. About 50 percent of black American children live in poverty. Many, if not most, of these children do not receive enough food to be healthy.

One group of Americans who cannot afford a proper diet go almost unnoticed. They belong to all races and ethnic groups. These are older people who are poor. You can see some of them in stores buying cat food or dog food. The only problem is that they may be buying it for themselves to eat. In some cases, elderly Americans starve quietly in their homes. In Boston, Loretta Schwartz-Nobel reports on the hardship of an elderly woman faced with hunger:

> On Friday, I held over two peas from the lunch. I ate one pea on Saturday morning. Then I got into bed with the taste of food in my mouth. . . . Later in the day I ate

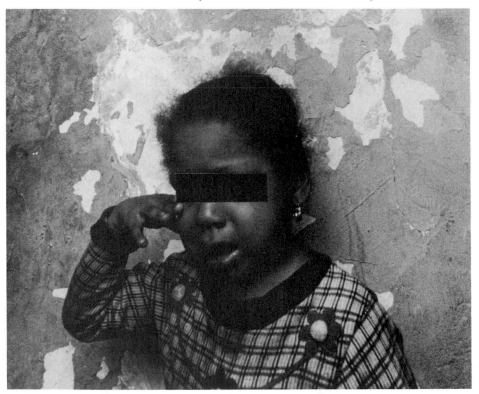

This girl in a slum in Washington, D.C., is brain damaged from eating lead paint.

the other pea. Today I saved the container that the mashed potatoes were in and tonight . . . I'll lick the sides of the container. When there are bones I keep them. . . . I boil the bones till they're soft and then I eat them. Today there were no bones.

In order to combat hunger and poverty in the United States, the government issues food stamps to qualified individuals and families. In order to receive food stamps, one must have a place of residence. Therefore, thousands of homeless Americans are unable to qualify. Rita Bermudez worked in an automobile factory. When she was laid off from her work with many other workers, Ms. Bermudez was asked to help hand out food to other laid-off workers. "We've had people that are living out of cars that had to give up their children because the money that we're getting from unemployment isn't enough to pay the rent and pay for the food and pay for the kids."

Although food stamps help many Americans in need, there are a number of problems. Some people use food stamps to pay rent. Of course, this is against the law, but there are landlords who will take food stamps at the rate of fifty cents on the dollar. That means if the rent is $100, the renter will pay $200, in food stamps. The landlord then must find someone to buy the food stamps. If the landlord sells the food stamps for sixty cents on the dollar, then he or she can make an additional $20 from the rent. In the end, the person on the food-stamp program loses $100. This is only one way in which food stamps are used illegally.

Another problem is that some people receive more food stamps than they should. This is usually done by having fake addresses and Social Security cards. One family working a food-stamp scheme took in $50,000 in one year. These rare practices often receive much attention and lead people who are not poor to support cutbacks in the food- stamp program. Actually, most of the people on food stamps are honest and really do need the assistance. Furthermore, being on welfare is not easy for many of these people. In another case, Ms. Bermudez describes how difficult it was for some people to ask for food.

> The husbands come in and they can't even say their names. We have to wait for 20 minutes to finally get the name out of this person and ask, "What's your name so we can help you?" They are on the verge of tears, these men.

In 1984, a group of doctors and health experts traveled throughout the United States in order to learn more about hunger among the people. They reported that no less than twenty million Americans suffer from hunger at some time during any month. The study of the doctors and health experts also reported that almost five hundred thousand children in the United States suffer from malnutrition.

Even with the food-stamp program, the amounts of money many people receive are not enough since there is no control over rent and other expenses. For example, Sister Marilyn Therese Rudy who works for a private organization that helps people in need recalled the following:

> . . . a woman we're working with right now: She has 2 children, ages 1½ years and 1 month. Her food stamp allocation is still only $76 a month. She has literally little or nothing to eat 15 days each month. We know because we visited her, she buys only food and pays her rent. We can't even help her to understand budgeting because she has no money to set aside.

Ending Hunger?

Although hunger is not something that will disappear tomorrow or the day after, the situation is far from hopeless. In the United States new aid programs have helped reduce hunger, and as people from all walks of life are becoming aware of the problem more is being done to help. The U.S. government and private groups have sent billions of dollars of food to needy countries which have provided at least temporary assistance.

Nevertheless, critics have noted that U.S. economic aid to other countries is generally limited to political allies. According to these critics, the United States should provide aid to those nations where it will do the most good. Some suggest that land of large landowners should be divided and distributed to poor farmers who currently are sharecroppers. In addition, political or military considerations, they argue, should not be the basis for providing aid. They also believe that the United States should do something to ensure that aid actually gets to the needy people. There is concern that much economic aid is misused by government officials in other nations for their own profit.

Other people point out, however, that economic assistance is a political tool used by almost all countries who provide aid. Thus, they argue that the United States should not be asked to help those who do not support the United States in return. In other words, they say why feed someone who bites your hand? As for the second notion that the United States should only assist those countries where it can be ensured that aid will reach the poor and needy, some point out that there are limits to how much a nation can or has the right to interfere in the internal politics of another nation.

As for land redistribution, this is a difficult task, and it does not always solve the problem. For example, during 1987 the Philippine government began distributing land to poor

187

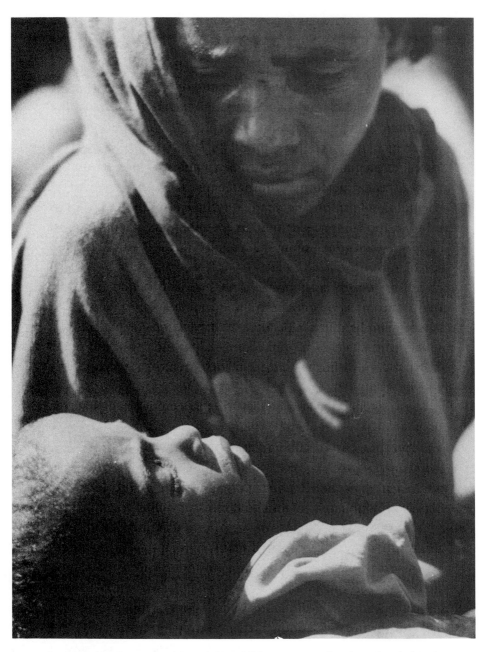

A young mother nurses her sickly child at a camp for drought victims in
Addis Ababa.

farmers. But as one farmer remarked to *The New York Times* writer, Seth Mydans, "Land does not grow, while families do." He explained that he has nine acres and nine children. When the children are grown, this will leave only one acre for each child. The problem of limited land and increasing population is not the only problem related to land reform. Another is the resistance of large landowners who do not want to lose their land. On the Philippine island of Negros, large plantation owners began to talk of breaking away from the Philippines and forming an independent state if the government attempted to redistribute land. "No one has the right to take away land belonging to someone else," complained a Negros landowner. The poor, however, claim that in the past, big powerful landowners have forced weaker farmers off their land. So, there is an ongoing argument as to who really owns the land. It is very apparent that simple solutions are not going to solve the problem of hunger in the Philippines and other struggling nations.

These issues are not easily resolved, and the debate continues. But what is very important is that the issues are being debated and people are becoming aware and showing concern for the problem of hunger. It is no longer being ignored or left up to individual nations as if they are isolated from the rest of the world.

The Green Revolution. There have been attempts to help improve the production of food by supplying countries with machinery and improved seeds that produce greater amounts of food crops. Scientific improvements in seed development and other technology or know-how to improve production has been called the green revolution. This green revolution has had some success in a number of places. In China, India, Mexico, Thailand, and many other countries the production of food has increased due to technological advances. The green revolution may be helpful in fighting hunger, but by itself it is not the final answer to the problem. As we have seen, there are many other problems of hunger over which the green revolution has no control.

Indeed, even within the green revolution there have been problems. Tractors and other major farm machinery are of great assistance to wealthy farm owners with large pieces of land. But, 90 percent of the world's farmers have land that is too small for large equipment. Therefore, the large landowners are able to produce more and drive the small landowner out of business.

The use of new varieties of seeds that produce new strains of rice or other crops sometimes results in crop failures. Small farmers cannot afford to lose a season's crop. For them, it means there will be little to eat until the next season. On the other hand, large landowners and international companies can risk a crop failure on part of their land without threatening their ability to survive. Finally, some improvements are designed to help increase production of cash crops that are sold to foreign countries and do not help the poor people who are undernourished in the producing country.

Francis Moore Lappé and Joseph Collins are the founders of the Food and Development Policy Institute, which is concerned with the study and elimination of world hunger. According to Lappé and Collins, the green revolution can help reduce world hunger if its advances can be applied by poor farmers as well as wealthy landowners and international companies. Nevertheless, new technology initially often benefits the more well-to-do. For example, the use of the automobile, television, air travel, and other conveniences were first used by those who could afford them. Today, such conveniences are used by people from all economic levels. Of course, these analogies or comparisons may not be perfect when applied to the question of hunger and the green revolution. Only time will tell.

Success Stories

It is important to realize that over the past decade or more there have been many success stories in regard to combatting the problem of hunger. These stories point to the fact that concerned citizens all over the world can help and are helping those who are less fortunate than themselves. Sometimes this help comes in the form of money or food; other times it comes in the form of badly needed tools, new technology, or volunteers who pitch in and actually work beside the local people. Among the successes that have taken place quite recently are the following:

- Forty-five recording artists—including Michael Jackson, Lionel Richie, Tina Turner, Bruce Springsteen, and Cyndi Lauper—raised more than $51 million singing and selling the recording 'We are the World.' All the money went to USA for Africa, an organization that spent or committed all of the money to buying food, medicine, and supplies for poor and hungry people in Ethiopia, the Sudan, and eight other African countries.

- To cut down on soil erosion, scientists have developed a cultivation system called "alley cropping." Crops such as corn, cowpeas, and yams are grown in four-yard-wide alleys separated by hedgerows of fast-growing trees or bushes. The hedgerows also can provide mulch, food for animals, stakes for climbing vines, and firewood.

- In villages near northern Cameroon, villagers and local private voluntary organizations have built sixteen wells which now provide clean water even during the worst part of the dry season.

- In northern Burkina Faso (formerly Upper Volta), the local people have erected small-scale earthen dams in order to be prepared for droughts.

- In Niger, private volunteer organizations are helping local women in a cooperative to improve their techniques for growing vegetables.

There are hundreds of other success stories like these. What is needed now is the concern of everybody everywhere to continue to contribute to such positive efforts.

> "Nobody made a greater mistake than he who did nothing because he could only do a little."
>
> —Edmund Burke, British Statesman (1729–1797)

8

Working to Protect Human Rights

Reactions vary among people when they hear or read about the violations of human rights. Some get extremely angry; others are deeply saddened. Still others try to ignore or quickly forget the stories. And then there are those who decide that they must do something, even if only a little, to help protect the human rights of all people all over the globe.

Can people, though, really do something to help others? Or are those who think they can help only fooling themselves? The fact is, plenty has been done and is being done by both individuals and groups to prevent or halt the deprivation of human rights.

As noted earlier in this book, there is ample proof that the work of human rights groups has actually saved people from being murdered. Further proof of this is the recent case in which a guard actually told a prisoner of conscience, "You are not dead because too many people are concerned about you." The guard was referring both to human rights activists and to those whom these activists had informed of the situation.

In another situation, a former torturer in El Salvador said, "If there was a lot of pressure—from human rights organizations or by some foreign countries—then we might pass the victim along to the judge. Otherwise, they were often killed."

Human rights organizations have also had a great amount of success in freeing prisoners of conscience from prison. For instance, Richard Stevens, a black South African who was imprisoned for his work against apartheid, has said that the letters Amnesty International (AI) sent to government officials ". . . made the Minister of Police actually visit the prison, show his face. The government does not ever want to admit they released somebody because of the pressure. But they do, they do. The officials would say, 'Who are these people writing to you? Why can't they leave us alone?'"

On yet another level, human rights organizations have succeeded in prodding governments and prison officials to treat political prisoners in a more humane way. For example, there is the case of Shahid Nadeem, a former political prisoner in Pakistan. Immediately after being arrested for organizing a workers' strike, Shahid was thrown in jail for a year. While imprisoned, he and the other inmates were forced to work in sweltering temperatures of up to 113° F (45° C). Furthermore, his cell was next to an open toilet filled with raw sewage, and the stench was so overwhelming he often could not get to sleep at night.

Then on June 9, 1978, he received a letter from a member of Amnesty International. It said, "You are not alone; don't lose heart. We pray for you. If there is anything you need, don't hesitate to ask." Upon receiving the letter Shahid said, "Suddenly I felt as if the sweat drops all over my body were drops from a cool, comforting shower. . . . The cell was no longer dark and suffocating." Within a short amount of time all of the other 1,200 prisoners heard about his letter from an

AI "adoption group" member in San Antonio, Texas. "My colleagues were overjoyed and their morale was suddenly high," he said.

That very night a prison official called Shahid into his office. "He was so friendly," Shahid says, "and respectful that I was shocked. He explained his dilemma as a God-fearing jailer who had to obey orders and follow the rules." Soon, however, the prison guards were "behaving themselves." Since then Shahid has often pondered over how "a woman from San Antonio had written some kind and comforting words which proved to be a bombshell for the prison authorities and significantly changed the prisoners' conditions for the better."

A former political prisoner from Vietnam has also testified as to how important the work of human rights organizations can be. "We could always tell," he has said, "when international protests were taking place. . . . the food rations increased and the beatings were fewer. Letters from abroad were translated and passed around from cell to cell, but when the letters stopped, the dirty food and repression started again."

Political prisoners are not the only ones who are helped by human rights activists and organizations; so are those who are denied their basic rights because of the color of their skin, the starving masses, and the poor and homeless refugees who scurry across borders in order to flee raging wars.

For example, the Free South Africa Movement has organized one antiapartheid protest after another in cities all over the United States in order to prod the American people to do something about the injustice of apartheid. Many of these protests have been held on U.S. college campuses such as Columbia University, Smith, Harvard, Rutgers, Yale, and the University of California at Berkeley.

As a result of these protests, numerous colleges have decided to divest or withdraw millions of dollars they have invested in stocks with companies that do business with and/or in South Africa. The aim of such an action is to put pressure on the South African government to change the unjust ways in which it treats its black population.

When asked whether such protests were of any help to his people, a black South African antiapartheid activist said: "Yes! Such protests in America are sending a message out all over the world that Americans care about the black person's situation in South Africa, and that Americans will not tolerate this modern style of slavery. The protests also give our people strength because it tells them that people in foreign places care about them. Finally, such actions are forcing the white government in South Africa to reconsider seriously the sagacity of keeping an entire people downtrodden. That is a start in the right direction—the direction toward freedom for black South Africans."

Throughout the world many relief agencies like UNICEF, the International Red Cross, Save the Children, and Oxfam rush tons of emergency supplies like food, water, and medicine to people who are either refugees from war-torn areas or suffering from starvation. UNICEF and organizations like the World Health Organization (WHO) are also involved in projects that assist the people in developing countries to help themselves. Such projects include both educational and health programs that teach people how to implement effective ways to boost food production, lower the frequency of infectious disease, and improve village sanitation.

While one person may only be able to do a little to help a political prisoner or a starving person, one should recognize that together with many other people a great deal can be accomplished. Knowing this often helps to keep up the spirits of those who work for the protection of human rights.

The Role of the United Nations

Over the past forty some years, the United Nations (UN) has played a major role in trying to protect people's human rights. The UN is an organization comprised of approximately two hundred nations that works for "world peace and the betterment of humanity." Countries from all over the world and with vastly different political beliefs are members of the UN.

As far as human rights are concerned, the UN's primary role has been in the development of a remarkable number of potentially important human rights documents. As mentioned in earlier chapters, these include the Universal Declaration of

A white South African woman protests laws in South Africa that force black families to live away from one another when a black man takes a job outside of his own town.

Human Rights; the Convention on the Prevention and Punishment of the Crime of Genocide; the International Covenant of Economic, Social, and Cultural Rights; and the International Convention on the Elimination of All Forms of Racial Discrimination, and others.

The ideas and goals in these documents have set international standards that humanity is expected to strive for in protecting everyone's human rights. And to a certain extent that has had a snowball effect. As more and more nations have begun to accept and adhere to these standards, this has placed

Grain is supplied by the World Food Program to people suffering from drought in Mozambique, Africa.

more pressure on other nations to fall in line and follow them.

But, as previously stated, that has only happened to a certain extent. As you have discovered by now, despite the examples of some nations, there are many that still ignore the ideals spelled out in the human rights documents and mistreat their citizens by depriving them of their human rights.

In these cases, the UN is limited in what it can do. While it can strongly encourage nations to follow the guidelines set out in the documents for protecting human rights, the UN does not have the power to force them to do so. As a result, it is in the area of making sure that all nations honor the rights of their citizens that the UN has been least successful.

Some nations and human rights activists think that the UN has not been as forceful as it could be in pressing other nations to respect their citizens' human rights. Basically they believe that the UN should be drawing as much attention as possible to those nations that torture, kill, and generally ill-treat their people. Others disagree, however, and claim that the UN can only do so much.

On another level, the UN has many special agencies that work for the betterment of humanity in the areas of agriculture, living and working conditions, health, and education. In doing so, they assist nations by helping them improve their farming and fishing procedures. They also provide needy countries with loans and other forms of aid like food, medical supplies, and shelter.

In those areas of the world that cannot afford to purchase enough food for their increasing populations, the UN supplies up to ten million tons of food per year. At the same time, the UN is also developing techniques to help control the ever-increasing population explosion in certain parts of the world. It also provides food to nations that have been hit by drought and famine.

Every year, throughout the world, millions of people

flee from wars, drought, famine, and floods. The UN helps these people, who are called refugees, by giving them food and shelter, trying to locate new homes for them, and by protecting their legal rights.

Finally, the UN carries out one of the largest human rights education programs in the world. It develops and distributes books and films on all sorts of human rights issues, and it also puts on seminars. In this way, it hopes to educate people about the importance of human rights, and to urge people to work for the protection of them.

What Individual Nations Can Do to Protect Their Citizens' Human Rights

As you have already learned, most nations have constitutions that guarantee protection of their citizens' basic human rights. Some nations like El Salvador, Haiti, Libya, and Syria even included parts of the UN's Universal Declaration of Human Rights in their own constitutions. This is the declaration that "expressed the hope that all humans would learn to respect the rights and dignity of all other humans."

Many nations seemingly strive as hard as possible to honor such promises. Others, however, treat some of their citizens so brutally that their constitutions' promises seem to be nothing more than cruel jokes.

How else can such constitutions be described when one discovers that some nations have death squads that torture, mutilate and kill opponents of the government? Or that in others, people are often jailed for months at a time, but never told why? Or that in still others there are political prisoners who have been found innocent of any wrongdoing but are still not allowed to go free or have been killed while being tortured?

Then there is the Soviet Union's constitution. While it

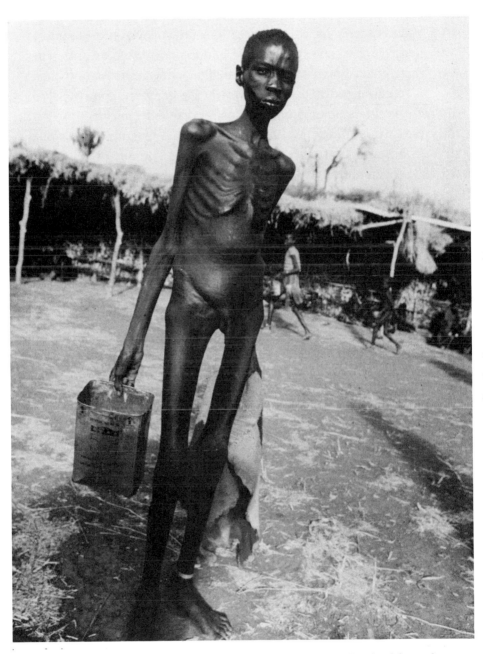

A severely malnourished person in Uganda waits to receive food from the United Nations.

"guarantees" its citizens freedom of speech and assembly, people are often severely punished for criticizing or protesting their government's policies. Finally, while it states that there is freedom of the press, the Soviet government controls all of the nation's newspapers, radios, and televisions. In this way, the Soviet authorities only allow what they want heard or read to be broadcast or printed.

Even those nations that strive hard to protect their citizens' rights often find it difficult to do so. In many cases, they often realize that if human rights are really going to be guaranteed for everyone, then something more than just words in a constitution will be needed. For example, they find that laws are often needed to enforce the protection of the rights. And even beyond that, they find that special agencies with special powers need to be established in order to make sure that the laws are carried out in a fair manner.

The black people's fight for their basic human rights in the United States provides a clear example of the above situation. For almost a hundred years following the Civil War, black Americans were treated as second-class citizens or worse. In most states they were not allowed to live in certain neighborhoods, and because of job discrimination they were forced to work at the most menial jobs. In many places they were not allowed to vote or to go to "white" schools.

But then, starting in the mid-1950s and continuing through the 1960s, many black people began protesting against their lack of freedom and rights. They demanded the same rights as other citizens—in education, housing, and employment. Eventually these protests forced the U.S. government, in 1957, to pass the first federal civil rights law since the end of the Civil War. The main purpose of this Civil Rights Act was to protect the rights of minority groups.

That act immediately set up an agency called the Commission on Civil Rights. Its main duty is to investigate cases in which people claim they have been denied their civil rights.

The act also created the Civil Rights Division in the Department of Justice. Its primary job is to enforce the civil rights and laws and regulations. Whenever a state, school, corporation, or other organization is found to be denying people their civil rights, this agency has the responsibility to correct immediately this unlawful action and/or prosecute the guilty parties.

All of these actions in the late 1950s were just the beginning of a major effort by the U.S. government to ensure that all of its citizens' civil rights were protected. The effort is still ongoing to this day.

The Use of Sanctions: Governments Pressuring
Other Governments to Protect Human Rights

Throughout the 1970s thousands of workers in various Polish cities flooded into the streets to protest the astronomical costs of food. Crying out that they could not afford to feed their families any longer on their paltry wages, the workers demanded that the government do something about it and do it fast. One protest ended when Polish government troops gunned down and murdered more than a hundred protesters.

Eventually such protests forced the Polish government to make numerous promises to improve daily life in Poland. These promises, however, were never fulfilled. As a result, life, for the most part, continued on as it had prior to the protests.

Then in the late 1970s the Polish workers formed a trade union. They believed that if they banded together they might have a chance to put pressure on the Polish government to be fairer to them. When the trade union called a strike, workers all over Poland stopped working. This included the shipyard workers, coal miners, steelworkers, bus drivers, writers, peasant farmers, firemen, and others.

In 1981, Polish authorities imposed martial law in order to halt the strike. This involved doing away with the regular laws and allowing the military to take over the country. The strike was then declared illegal, the union was crushed, and the union leaders were jailed. Many Poles began to feel like their country had become one huge prison.

Many nations across the world protested the Polish government's use of martial law and called on the Polish leaders to lift it. When Poland refused to free the union leaders or lift martial law, some nations decided to impose economic sanctions. Economic sanctions are measures that are sometimes adopted by one nation (or several nations together) in order to force another country to stop violating international laws. In this case, certain nations wanted to force Poland to honor its citizens' human rights.

The United States was one of the nations that imposed economic sanctions against Poland in 1981. In doing so, it placed restrictions on U.S. trade with Poland and worked to prevent Poland from getting badly needed loans from the World Bank. The U.S. said that before the sanctions would be dropped, Poland would have to lift martial law and free its political prisoners.

Even though it took the Polish government several years to meet the demands of the U.S., the sanctions paid off. In 1983, Poland lifted martial law. Then in 1986 it freed most of its political prisoners. Many experts say that if the United States had not imposed the sanctions, the prisoners would not have been freed at that time.

Poland is not the only nation that has faced economic sanctions for denying its people their basic human rights. For instance, since 1985 South Africa has also been hit with a flurry of economic as well as political sanctions as a protest against its racist system of apartheid.

Many in the world believe that apartheid is a major violation of human rights, and that it should be abolished. That is why many nations (including the United States, Great Britain, and France as well as others), at least nineteen U.S. states, sixty-five cities, and more than forty universities have all imposed some type of economic sanctions on South Africa. Furthermore, over thirty major U.S. companies have totally quit doing business with that nation because of apartheid.

So far all of these sanctions have not forced South Africa to do away with apartheid, but those in favor of the sanctions are not worried. They feel that the ongoing and mounting pressure on South Africa will eventually result in the abolition of apartheid. Only time will tell.

The Role of Nongovernmental Human Rights Groups

"What does it say about me as a human being if I know there are injustices in the world and do nothing to remedy them?" Those are the words of a human rights activist who has dedicated many years of his life to working for the protection of human rights. The question he has posed could well serve as the motto for tens of thousands of people who have worked with nongovernmental human rights organizations (NGOs).

A nongovernmental human rights organization is one that is not affiliated with any government. It is an organization that is made up of private individuals like you, your parents and teachers who are extremely concerned about human rights and wish to help those who are being denied theirs.

Throughout the world there are literally hundreds of nongovernmental groups that work for the protection of human rights. Some like Amnesty International primarily work on the behalf of political prisoners. Others like Oxfam, Bread for the World, and the Hunger Project work to prevent people from starving or suffering from malnutrition. Such groups as

Schoolchildren in Upper Volta, Africa, line up to receive milk provided by the government.

Survival International, the Indian Rights Group, and Cultural Survival try to protect the lives and cultures of indigenous peoples—people like the Bushmen in southern Africa and the Aboriginals in Australia. Other groups focus in on protecting people from racial discrimination, genocide, torture, censorship, and so on.

Some human rights groups strictly do research on human rights problems. They dig and probe into problems and then write reports on their findings. These reports are often used by other human rights groups as well as some governments in order to protect human rights or to protest human rights violations. Still other groups concentrate on educating the public and government officials about human rights violations. At the same time, these groups urge people to get involved in helping those who are being deprived of their rights.

Then there are those organizations that actually carry out projects to help individuals and groups of people who are in need of help. Such projects are extremely diverse: collecting and shipping tons of food to starving people in Africa and Asia, setting up temporary camps and providing medical help to refugees, halting torture of people. Some organizations, it should be noted, are involved in all three types of work mentioned above.

These organizations realize, as Thomas Hammarberg (a human rights activist) has pointed out, that the governments who deny their people human rights depend on "ignorance and indifference among both the citizens in their country and public abroad." In essence, each group is working against that very situation. Each in its own way is working to educate people about human rights violations and to get them to care about such problems.

What Individuals Can Do

Over six hundred years ago, the Italian poet Dante claimed

that "He who sees, stands by, and does nothing as evil is performed, is just as guilty as he who performs it." Just this sort of thought has prompted many "ordinary" citizens to become active in protecting other peoples' human rights.

As previously mentioned, there are literally hundreds of human rights groups one could join. It really depends on what issue one wishes to work on—preventing torture, saving starving people, working for the release of political prisoners, halting racism, preventing genocide, and so on.

Amnesty International is one of the most famous human rights organizations, and it is also one whose members know they can make a difference in the world by promoting the protection of human rights.

For instance, a former political prisoner from Uruguay wrote the following about the work of Amnesty members: "The task that you have been carrying out for years is a hand stretched out further than the iron bars of prison, which in our worst moments makes us feel that we are never alone."

Amnesty members never take credit for freeing prisoners because, as they point out, "many factors may enter into a government's decision to free someone." Amnesty points out, "it [the organization] is concerned with getting results, not with getting credit."

All around the world Amnesty International has set up what it calls "adoption groups," or local chapters. Each local chapter is comprised of between ten and twenty-five people who live near one another. As soon as a local chapter group is formed, it is given the cases of three political prisoners by AI headquarters in England.

To ensure that its work is always fair and impartial, each AI group works for individual prisoners of conscience who not only have different political or religious beliefs but who come from different countries. In that way, no one can fairly

A human rights activist protests the abuse of human rights in Chile.

accuse AI of criticizing any one type of government or only working for prisoners with certain beliefs or from certain countries.

The most important job of the adoption groups is to work for the release of its political prisoners. It does this primarily by writing letter after letter that call on governments to release the prisoners.

As Scott Harrison, a longtime AI worker, has said, "We've been writing letters for 25 years, and we continue to do it because it's an effective way to stop human rights abuses."

How, though, can letters be effective in this way? Basically the officials of the countries that receive the letters suddenly realize that people all over the world are watching their actions, and making them public. This often concerns the leaders for a number of different reasons. First, it is a fact of international politics that most nations desire to look good and just, even if they are not, in the eyes of the world. Second, the officials often become concerned that the negative publicity they are receiving may damage their political relationships with other nations. Third, they may be afraid that such publicity may also hurt their economy by bringing on economic sanctions against their nation.

Julio de Peña Caldez, a former political prisoner in the Dominican Republic, has testified as to how much pressure such letters can put on a government. He has said, "When the first two hundred letters came, the guards gave me back my clothes. Then the next two hundred came, and the prison director came to see me. When the next pile of letters arrived, the director got in touch with his superior. The letters kept coming and coming: three thousand of them. The president was informed. The letters still kept arriving, and the president called the prison and told them to let me go.

"After I was released, the president called me into his office for a man-to-man talk. He said: 'How is it that a trade union leader like you has so many friends all over the world?' He showed me an enormous box full of letters he had received, and when we parted, he gave them to me. I still have them."

It has been claimed that Mr. Caldez may never have been freed if people had ignored his plight. However, thousands of people did not ignore his situation and instead wrote letters calling for his release. And they were successful. The point is, one individual, along with many others, can make a tremendous difference in the world.

In regard to the problem of world hunger, many people— including Americans—voluntarily travel to places like Africa in order to help the starving masses. Some people work on their own, while others belong to groups like the International Red Cross, the World Food Program, or Oxfam. Among the professions represented by the volunteers are economists, doctors, nutritionists, engineers, warehouse and seaport managers, foresters, mechanics, and secretaries. Over time these volunteers have picked up such strange nicknames as "masters of disasters," "relief chiefs," and "famine legionnaires."

The work such people do depends on both the skills they have as well as a country's needs. Some of the many jobs they engage in are dishing food out to the hungry, providing medical attention to the ill, digging water holes, transporting the food across deserts and war zones, and educating the local inhabitants about new and more efficient ways to farm.

Dr. Nancy L. Caroline is one of the volunteers who has dedicated her life to finding a way to prevent people from starving in Africa. In doing so, she is developing a 5,000-acre cooperative farm on which she will teach people in Kenya how to grow crops using new and unique farming methods.

Mozambican children receive food rations at a special center in Zimbabwe, Africa. Over fifty thousand Mozambicans crossed the border fleeing drought and starvation in their own country.

One of her main goals is to teach the people how to keep the land fertile with small amounts of water and to prevent the land from being taken over by the desert. Of her work she has said: "I have seen children die from starvation right before my eyes, and I finally came to the conclusion that while free medicine and food are necessary for starving people, they only go so far in really helping the people. I now think that if people learn how to use the land more efficiently they will be able to halt some of the conditions that lead to drought and, ultimately, starvation."

Still other individuals remain in the United States in order to help feed the hungry in our nation. Pat Trouth, a member of the Hunger Project, is one such person. When she learned from a friend that a company in Philadelphia, Pennsylvania, had $30,000 worth of canned soup sitting unused in a warehouse, she convinced the company to donate the soup to the Washington, D.C. Food Bank, which distributes food to soup kitchens that feed poor people.

In Seattle, Washington, three people—Doris and Allan Henderson and Ellas Renton—decided to do something to help the hungry people in their community and did so by collecting tons of food and creating a food bank. Once the food was collected, they passed it out on a regular basis to people who could not afford enough food for themselves or their families.

Pam Milchrist, a professor of physical education at California State University at Sacramento, has a special place in her heart for refugees who have fled war zones. She has taken off work several times and paid her own way to Thailand in order to help the refugee children who survived the mass killings by the Khmer Rouge in Kampuchea.

She gets the kids involved in physical activities and games in order to both improve their health as well as their mental outlook. In regard to her work Milchrist said: "In any child's development he or she needs to play and what the kids in the Kampuchean refugee camps needed more than anything else was to be kids again. For a long time they were too sick and too wounded emotionally to do anything other than sit and stare off into space. Just stare. Some had lost their entire family. Gradually I got them to play. In a sense I was bringing them back to life."

What You Can Do
There are numerous ways in which an individual can work for the protection of human rights. Among the many ways are the following: taking part in a food or clothing drive for the needy, passing around and/or signing petitions that call on a government to free its political prisoners, contributing money or fund-raising for a human rights group, or joining a human rights organization.

Oxfam-America, a group that works to prevent world hunger, has numerous activities that students can work on in order to aid the organization. One way is to conduct a school assembly on world hunger to teach other students about the ordeals many people are facing throughout the world.

Another project that Oxfam suggests is for students to organize a recycling center in which they collect material such as aluminum, steel, glass, and paper. This not only helps to conserve resources and to clean up the environment, but the material can be sold and the funds can be donated to Oxfam or other groups that try to prevent hunger.

One kindergarten class in Brookline, Massachusetts, designed its own calendar with the help of a local printer, and then sold it and raised over a thousand dollars for Oxfam.

Bread for the World, another group that is working to prevent hunger, also has activities in which students can participate. For example, a high school in New York City has participated in a yearly walkathon to raise funds for Bread for the World. The first year, 75 students took part in the twenty-mile walk. The second year 150 students participated, and the third year over 200 students raised over three thousand five hundred dollars. The walkathon has helped to bring the students and faculty members together in a common project to make people aware of world hunger and to raise money for those working on behalf of the hungry.

As for joining an organization, Amnesty International has campus adoption groups. These are made up of students and their teachers, and they basically do the same work as local chapters.

In addition to writing letters to governments asking for the release of political prisoners, the students also take part in many AI activities. Such activities include writing articles for school and community newspapers, appearing on local radio and television programs and talking about their human rights work, holding vigils outside foreign embassies, collecting signatures on international petitions, and raising money to help political prisoners.

Many students find their work in campus groups fascinating as well as educational. As one high-school student in Washington, D.C., said: "For the first time, really, learning about geography and politics and stuff like that seemed important and not a waste of time. I mean, now I was learning all of this stuff, not because I had to take a test but because I cared about what was happening to our prisoners of conscience in another part of the world."

By working on human rights issues many students have found that reaching out and helping others can be extremely satisfying. They have also found out that Edmund Burke was right when he said, "Nobody made a greater mistake than he who did nothing because he could only do a little."

A Brief Listing of Some of the Genocidal Acts That have Occurred During the Twentieth Century

YEAR   EVENT

*1904   The German government massacred 65,000 (out of a population of 80,000) people known as the Hereros in southern Africa.

*1915   The Ottomans (Turkish) killed at least a million Armenian people in an attempt to "destroy completely all of the Armenians living in Turkey."

*1919   The Ukrainians slaughtered between 100,000 to 250,000 Jews in 2,000 different pogroms (massacres).

1932–33   The Soviet Union, under Josef Stalin, purposely starved to death as many as ten million Ukrainian people.

1936–39   At least 400,000 to 500,000 people were shot and killed in the Soviet Union for political reasons. In 1937–38 there were days when up to a thousand people were shot in Moscow alone.

*1941–45   The Nazi Holocaust in Europe resulted in the slaughter of approximately six million Jewish people. The ultimate aim of the Holocaust was to murder every last Jew on earth.

At this same time, the Nazis also planned to exterminate the group known as Gypsies. By 1945 half a million Gypsies had been slaughtered by the Nazis.

1943–46	During this time Russia, under the dictatorship of Stalin, deported whole nations of people from their native lands. These included the Karachai and the Autonomous Kalmyk Republic, the Chechen and Ingush peoples, and all Balkans. Many of the exiles died even before arriving at their destinations. The survivors were treated extremely harshly in order to bring about their destruction.
1950–59	China attempted to annihilate Buddhism in Tibet.
1965	The government of Indonesia slaughtered up to 600,000 people it accused of being "communists." Many of these people were simply opponents of the government.
1965–72	The Tutsi killed between 100,000 to 300,000 people of the Hutu tribe in the African nation of Burundi.
1965–present	More than one hundred thousand peasant Indians in Guatemala have been killed by the Guatemalan military troops.
1966	Whole tribes of the Ibo people were massacred in northern Nigeria by government troops.
1971	The Pakistan government killed between one to three million Bengalis.
*1972–73	The Paraguayan government enslaved, tortured, and killed thousands of Ache Indians in Paraguay.
*1975–79	Hundreds of thousands of Kampuchean people were killed in a series of purges by Khmer Rouge. Even more people died on forced labor marches. Altogether, between

	one to three million people were killed.
1975–present	An estimated 100,000 citizens (out of a population of 600,000) of East Timor have been slain by Indonesian troops.
1980–present	Hundreds of members of the Bahá'í religion have been tortured and executed in Iran under the government of Ayatollah Khomeini.

Chronology Footnote

* An asterisk appears by those dates and incidences that the *United Nations Report on Genocide* (July 2, 1985) notes as examples of genocide in the twentieth century. The other mass killings were not identified as genocide in the UN report because the UN Genocide Convention and Treaty do not include political massacres under their definitions of genocide.

Nevertheless, it should be noted that many scholars think that political massacres, purges, and pogroms should also be officially considered genocide.

> *On 10 December 1948*, the General Assembly of the United Nations acopted and proclaimed the Universal Declaration of Human Rights, the full text of which appears in the following pages. Following this historic act, the Assembly called upon all Member countries to publicize the text of the Declaration and "to cause it to be disseminated, displayed, read and expounded principally in schools and other educational institutions, without distinction based on the political status of countries or territories".

Javier Pérez de Cuéllar
SECRETARY-GENERAL

Universal
Declaration
of
Human Rights

**United Nations
Department of Public Information**

Universal Declaration of Human Rights

Preamble

Whereas recognition of the inherent dignity and of the equal and inalienable rights of all members of the human family is the foundation of freedom, justice and peace in the world,

Whereas disregard and contempt for human rights have resulted in barbarous acts which have outraged the conscience of mankind, and the advent of a world in which human beings shall enjoy freedom of speech and belief and freedom from fear and want has been proclaimed as the highest aspiration of the common people,

Whereas it is essential, if man is not to be compelled to have recourse, as a last resort, to rebellion against tyranny and oppression, that human rights should be protected by the rule of law,

Whereas it is essential to promote the development of friendly relations between nations,

Whereas the peoples of the United Nations have in the Charter reaffirmed their faith in fundamental human rights, in the dignity and worth of the human person and in the equal rights of men and women and have deter-

All human beings are born with equal and inalienable rights and fundamental freedoms.

The United Nations is committed to upholding, promoting and protecting the human rights of every individual. This commitment stems from the United Nations Charter, which reaffirms the faith of the peoples of the world in fundamental human rights and in the dignity and worth of the human person.

In the Universal Declaration of Human Rights, the United Nations has stated in clear and simple terms the rights which belong equally to every person.

These rights belong to you.

They are your rights.

Familiarize yourself with them. Help to promote and defend them for yourself as well as for your fellow human beings.

...mined to promote social progress and better standards of life in larger freedom,

Whereas Member States have pledged themselves to achieve, in co-operation with the United Nations, the promotion of universal respect for and observance of human rights and fundamental freedoms,

Whereas a common understanding of these rights and freedoms is of the greatest importance for the full realization of this pledge,

Now, Therefore,

The General Assembly

proclaims

This Universal Declaration of Human Rights

as a common standard of achievement for all peoples and all nations, to the end that every individual and every organ of society, keeping this Declaration constantly in mind, shall strive by teaching and education to promote respect for these rights and freedoms and by progressive measures, national and international, to secure their universal and effective recognition and observance, both among the peoples of Member States themselves and among the peoples of territories under their jurisdiction.

Article 1

All human beings are born free and equal in dignity and rights. They are endowed with reason and conscience and should act towards one another in a spirit of brotherhood.

Article 2

Everyone is entitled to all the rights and freedoms set forth in this Declaration, without distinction of any kind, such as race, colour, sex, language, religion, political or other opinion, national or social origin, property, birth or other status.

Furthermore, no distinction shall be made on the basis of the political, jurisdictional or international status of the country or territory to which a person belongs, whether it be independent, trust, non-selfgoverning or under any other limitation of sovereignty.

Article 3

Everyone has the right to life, liberty and security of person.

Article 4

No one shall be held in slavery or servitude; slavery and the slave trade shall be prohibited in all their forms.

Article 5

No one shall be subjected to torture or to cruel, inhuman or degrading treatment or punishment.

Article 6

Everyone has the right to recognition everywhere as a person before the law.

Article 7

All are equal before the law and are entitled without any discrimination to equal protection of the law. All are entitled to equal protection against any discrimination in violation of this Declaration and against any incitement to such discrimination.

Article 8

Everyone has the right to an effective remedy by the competent national tribunals for acts violating the fundamental rights granted him by the constitution or by law.

Article 9

No one shall be subjected to arbitrary arrest, detention or exile.

Article 10

Everyone is entitled in full equality to a fair and public hearing by an independent and impartial tribunal, in the determination of his rights and obligations and of any criminal charge against him.

Article 11

(1) Everyone charged with a penal offence has the right to be presumed innocent until proved guilty ac-

cording to law in a public trial at which he has had all the guarantees necessary for his defence.

(2) No one shall be held guilty of any penal offence on account of any act or omission which did not constitute a penal offence, under national or international law, at the time when it was committed. Nor shall a heavier penalty be imposed than the one that was applicable at the time the penal offence was committed.

Article 12

No one shall be subjected to arbitrary interference with his privacy, family, home or correspondence, nor to attacks upon his honour and reputation. Everyone has the right to the protection of the law against such interference or attacks.

Article 13

(1) Everyone has the right to freedom of movement and residence within the borders of each State.

(2) Everyone has the right to leave any country, including his own, and to return to his country.

Article 14

(1) Everyone has the right to seek and to enjoy in other countries asylum from persecution.

(2) This right may not be invoked in the case of prosecutions genuinely arising from non-political

crimes or from acts contrary to the purposes and principles of the United Nations.

Article 15

(1) Everyone has the right to a nationality.

(2) No one shall be arbitrarily deprived of his nationality nor denied the right to change his nationality.

Article 16

(1) Men and women of full age, without any limitation due to race, nationality or religion, have the right to marry and to found a family. They are entitled to equal rights as to marriage, during marriage and at its dissolution.

(2) Marriage shall be entered into only with the free and full consent of the intending spouses.

(3) The family is the natural and fundamental group unit of society and is entitled to protection by society and the State.

Article 17

(1) Everyone has the right to own property alone as well as in association with others.

(2) No one shall be arbitrarily deprived of his property.

Article 18

Everyone has the right to freedom of thought, conscience and religion; this right includes freedom to change his religion or belief, and freedom, either alone or in community with others and in public or private, to manifest his religion or belief in teaching, practice, worship and observance.

Article 19

Everyone has the right to freedom of opinion and expression; this right includes freedom to hold opinions without interference and to seek, receive and impart information and ideas through any media and regardless of frontiers.

Article 20

(1) Everyone has the right to freedom of peaceful assembly and association.

(2) No one may be compelled to belong to an association.

Article 21

(1) Everyone has the right to take part in the government of his country, directly or through freely chosen representatives.

(2) Everyone has the right of equal access to public service in his country.

Article 22

Everyone, as a member of society, has the right to social security and is entitled to realization, through national effort and international co-operation and in accordance with the organization and resources of each State, of the economic, social and cultural rights indispensable for his dignity and the free development of his personality.

Article 23

(1) Everyone has the right to work, to free choice of employment, to just and favourable conditions of work and to protection against unemployment.

(2) Everyone, without any discrimination, has the right to equal pay for equal work.

(3) Everyone who works has the right to just and favourable remuneration ensuring for himself and his family an existence worthy of human dignity, and supplemented, if necessary, by other means of social protection.

(4) Everyone has the right to form and to join trade unions for the protection of his interests.

Article 24

Everyone has the right to rest and leisure, including reasonable limitation of working hours and periodic holidays with pay.

Article 25

(1) Everyone has the right to a standard of living adequate for the health and well-being of himself and of his family, including food, clothing, housing and medical care and necessary social services, and the right to security in the event of unemployment, sickness, disability, widowhood, old age or other lack of livelihood in circumstances beyond his control.

(2) Motherhood and childhood are entitled to special care and assistance. All children, whether born in or out of wedlock, shall enjoy the same social protection.

Article 26

(1) Everyone has the right to education. Education shall be free, at least in the elementary and fundamental stages. Elementary education shall be compulsory. Technical and professional education shall be made generally available and higher education shall be equally accessible to all on the basis of merit.

(2) Education shall be directed to the full development of the human personality and to the strengthening of respect for human rights and fundamental

(3) The will of the people shall be the basis of the authority of government; this will shall be expressed in periodic and genuine elections which shall be by universal and equal suffrage and shall be held by secret vote or by equivalent free voting procedures.

freedoms. It shall promote understanding, tolerance and friendship among all nations, racial or religious groups, and shall further the activities of the United Nations for the maintenance of peace.

(3) Parents have a prior right to choose the kind of education that shall be given to their children.

Article 27

(1) Everyone has the right freely to participate in the cultural life of the community, to enjoy the arts and to share in scientific advancement and its benefits.

(2) Everyone has the right to the protection of the moral and material interests resulting from any scientific, literary or artistic production of which he is the author.

Article 28

Everyone is entitled to a social and international order in which the rights and freedoms set forth in this Declaration can be fully realized.

Article 29

(1) Everyone has duties to the community in which alone the free and full development of his personality is possible.

(2) In the exercise of his rights and freedoms, everyone shall be subject only to such limitations as are determined by law solely for the purpose of securing

227

due recognition and respect for the rights and freedoms of others and of meeting the just requirements of morality, public order and the general welfare in a democratic society.

(3) These rights and freedoms may in no case be exercised contrary to the purposes and principles of the United Nations.

Article 30

Nothing in this Declaration may be interpreted as implying for any State, group or person any right to engage in any activity or to perform any act aimed at the destruction of any of the rights and freedoms set forth herein.

Human Rights Organizations

Americas Watch, 36 West 44th Street, New York, NY 10036

Amnesty International, 322 Eighth Avenue, New York, NY 10001

Bread for the World, 801 Rhode Island Avenue, NE, Washington, DC 20018

Cultural Survival, Inc., 11 Divinity Avenue, Cambridge, MA 02138

Facing History and Ourselves, 25 Kennard Road, Brookline, MA 02146

Freedom House, 20 West 40th Street, New York, NY 10018

Helsinki Watch, 36 West 44th Street, Room 911, New York, NY 10036

Institute of the International Conference on the Holocaust and Genocide, POB 10311, Jerusalem 93624, Israel

International Alert, 1580 Massachusetts Avenue, #7F, Cambridge, MA 02138

Minority Rights Group, 29 Craven Street, London WC2, England

Survival International (USA), 2121 Decatur Place, NW, Washington, DC 20008

United Nations Centre Against Apartheid, Room 2775-C, United Nations, New York, NY 10027

United States Holocaust Memorial Council, 425 13th Street NW, Suite 832, Washington, DC 20004

Washington Office on Africa, 110 Maryland Avenue, NE, Washington, DC 20002

Washington Office on Latin America, 110 Maryland Avenue, NE, Washington, DC 20002

Zachor: The Holocaust Resource Center, 250 West 57th Street, Suite 216, New York, NY 10019

Further Reading

Nonfiction: Books and Reports

Altshuler, David A. *Hitler's War Against the Jews*. New York: Behrman House, 1982.

Amnesty International. *Amnesty International 1986*. London: Amnesty International, 1988.

————*Prisoners of Conscience*. London: Amnesty International, 1981.

Amnesty International USA.

Conscience and Human Rights: An Amnesty International Curriculum. *San Francisco: Amnesty International USA, 1981.*

————*Disappearances: A Workbook*. New York: Amnesty International USA, 1981.

————*High School Curriculum on Torture*. San Francisco: Amnesty International USA, 1983.

————*Political Killings by Governments*. New York: Amnesty International USA, 1983.

Anti-Defamation League of B'nai B'rith. *The Record: The Holocaust in History, 1933–1945*. New York: Anti-Defamation League, 1978.

Archer, Jules. *You Can't Do That To Me! Famous Fights for Human Rights*. New York: Macmillan, 1980.

Brown, Dee. *Bury My Heart at Wounded Knee: An Indian History of the American West*. New York: Holt, Rinehart, Winston, 1970.

Cantarow, Ellen. *Moving the Mountain: Women Working for Social Change*. Old Westbury, NY: Feminist Press, 1980.

Carrigan, Ana. *Salvador Witness: The Life and Calling of Jean Donovan*. New York: Simon and Schuster, 1984.

Chartok, Roselle, and Jack Spencer. *The Holocaust Years: Society on Trial*. New York: Bantam, 1978.

de Kay, J. T. *Meet Martin Luther King, Jr.* New York: Random House, 1969.

Dobrin, Arthur, Lynn Dobrin, and Thomas F. Liotti. *Convictions: Political Prisoners—Their Stories*. Maryknoll, NY: Orbis Books, 1981.

Fisher, Dorothea Canfield. *A Fair World for All: The Meaning of the Declaration of Human Rights*. New York: McGraw-Hill, 1952.

Foreign Policy Study Foundation. *South Africa: Time Running Out*. Berkeley: University of California Press, 1981.

Frank, Anne. *Anne Frank: Diary of a Young Girl*. New York: Doubleday, 1967.

232

Griffin, John Howard. *Black Like Me*. New York: New American Library, 1976.

Haskins, James. *The Life and Death of Martin Luther King, Jr.* New York: Lothrop, 1977.

Hauser, Thomas. *Missing*. New York: Avon, 1982.

Hautzig, Esther. *The Endless Steppe*. New York: Crowell, 1968.

Kherdian, David. *The Road from Home: The Story of an Armenian Girl*. New York: Greenwillow, 1979.

Larsen, Egon. *A Flame in Barbed Wire: The Story of Amnesty International*. New York: Norton, 1977.

Laure, Jason, and Ettagale Laure. *South Africa: Coming of Age Under Apartheid*. New York: Farrar, 1980.

Lester, Elenore. *Wallenberg: The Man in the Iron Web*. New York: Prentice-Hall, 1980.

Lester, Julius. *To Be a Slave*. New York: Dial, 1968.

Levin, Leah. *Human Rights: Questions and Answers*. Paris: The UNESCO Press, 1981.

McKown, Robin. *Seven Famous Trials in History*. New York: Vanguard, 1963.

Power, Jonathan. *Amnesty International: The Human Rights Story*. New York: McGraw-Hill, 1981.

Savage, Katherine. *The Story of the United Nations*. New York: Walch, 1970.

Tateishi, John. *And Justice for All: An Oral History of the Japanese American Detention Camps*. New York: Random House, 1984.

Terzina, James P., and Kathryn Cramer. *Mighty Hard Road: The Story of Cesar Chavez.* New York: Doubleday, 1970.

United Nations. *Human Rights: 50 Questions and Answers About Human Rights and United Nations Activities to Promote Them.* New York: United Nations Publications, 1980.

United Nations Centre Against Apartheid. *A Crime Against Humanity. Questions and Answers on Apartheid in South Africa.* New York: United Nations Centre Against Apartheid, 1980.

Whitney, Sharon. *Eleanor Roosevelt.* New York: Watts, 1982.

Wiesel, Elie. *Night.* New York: Bantam, 1982.

Wright, Richard. *Black Boy.* 1945. Reprint. New York: Harper & Row, 1969.

Fiction: Novels, Plays, and Short Stories

Bradbury, Ray. *Farenheit 451.* New York: Ballantine, 1971.

Butler, William. *Butterfly Revolution.* New York: Ballantine, 1975.

Demetz, Hana. *The House on Prague Street.* Boston: G.K. Hall, 1980.

Henderson, Nancy. *Walk Together: Five Plays on Human Rights.* New York: Messner, 1974.

Huxley, Aldous. *Brave New World.* New York: Penguin, 1974.

Miller, Arthur. *The Crucible.* New York: Penguin, 1974.

Orwell, George. *Animal Farm.* New York: Penguin, 1973.

——*1984.* New York: Penguin, 1975.

Rand, Ayn. *Anthem*. New York: Signet, 1975.

Solzhenitsyn, Alexander. *One Day in the Life of Ivan Denisovich*. New York: Penguin, 1977.

Steiner, Jean-François. *Treblinka*. New York: New American Library, 1979.

West, Morris. *Proteus*. New York: Bantam, 1980.

References

Chapter One

Amnesty International USA. *Political Killings by Governments*. New York: Amnesty International USA, 1983.

Branson, Margaret Stimmann, and Judith Torney-Purta *International Human Rights, Society, and the Schools*. Washington, D.C.: National Council for the Social Studies, 1982.

Connecticut State Department of Education. *Human Rights: The Struggle for Freedom, Dignity and Equality*. Hartford, CT: Connecticut State Department of Education, 1986.

"Escape to W. Berlin Reportedly Foiled." *Sacramento Bee*. July 1, 1986.

Fireside, Harvey. *Soviet Psychoprisons*. New York: W.W. Norton & Company, 1979.

Gastil, Raymond D., ed. *Freedom in the World: Political Rights and Civil Liberties, 1983–84*. New York: Freedom House, 1984.

Levin, Leah. *Human Rights: Questions and Answers*. Paris: The Unesco Press, 1981.

Reardon, Betty. *Human Rights*. Philadelphia, PA: The World Affairs Council of Philadelphia, 1978.

Schumacher, Edward. "Breaking Silence on Argentina's 'Missing'." *The New York Times*, April 4, 1982.

Toronto Arts Group for Human Rights. *The Writer and Human Rights*. Garden City, NY: Anchor Press, 1982.

Totten, Samuel, ed. *Social Education* (Special issue: "Teaching About International Human Rights.") September 1985.

United Nations. *Human Rights: 50 Questions and Answers About Human Rights and United Nations Activities to Promote Them*. New York: United Nations Publications, 1980.

United States Department of State. *Country Reports on Human Rights Practices for 1985*. Washington, D.C.: U.S. Government Printing Office, 1986.

Chapter Two

Amnesty International. *Conscience and Human Rights: An Amnesty International Curriculum.* San Francisco: Amnesty International USA and Coastal Ridge Research and Education Center, 1979.

Branson, Margaret Stimmann, and Judith Torney-Purts. *International Human Rights, Society, and the Schools.* Washington, D.C.: National Council for the Social Studies, 1982.

Brown, Dee. *Bury My Heart at Wounded Knee: An Indian History of the American West.* New York: Holt, Rinehart Winston, 1970.

Chief Joseph. "An Indian's View of Indian Affairs." *North American Review,* vol. 128 (1879), p. 417.

Connecticut State Department of Education. *Human Rights: The Struggle for Freedom, Dignity and Equality.* Hartford, CT: Connecticut State Department of Education, 1986.

"Dachau Captured by Americans, Who Kill Guards, Liberate 32,000." *The New York Times,* April 30, 1945.

"Down and Out in L.A." *Time,* June 22, 1987.

Lash, Joseph P. *Eleanor: The Years Alone,* New York: Norton, 1972.

Levin, Leah. *Human Rights: Questions and Answers.* Paris: The UNESCO Press, 1981.

Roosevelt, Eleanor. *The Autobiography of Eleanor Roosevelt.* New York: Harper & Brothers, 1958, p. 322.

Schlafly, Phyllis. *The Power of the Positive Women.* New York: Jove Publications, 1981, p. 99.

"Torture as Policy: The Network of Evil." August 16, 1976. *Time* (European Edition).

U.S. Congress. 39th. 2nd Session. *Senate Report 156.* pp. 73, 96.

Chapter Three

Allport, Gordon. *The Nature of Prejudice.* Cambridge, Mass.: Addison-Wesley, 1954.

Carlson, Joel. *No Neutral Ground.* New York: Thomas Y. Crowell, 1973.

Daniel, W. W. *Racial Discrimination in England: Based upon the PEP Report.* Baltimore: Penguin, 1968, pp. 74–75, 78–79.

Dushnyck, Walter. "Discrimination and Abuse of Power in the USSR." *Case Studies on Human Rights and Fundamental Freedoms: A World Survey,* ed. Willem A. Veenhoven. The Hague: Martinus Nijhoff, 1975, p. 465.

Greer, William R. "City Police Have Changed Their Approach to Family Disputes." *The New York Times,* May 25, 1985, p. 15.

Hiemer, Ernst. *Der Giftpilz.* Nuremberg: Der Stuermer, 1938.

Hovey, Gail, and Sarah Munson. "Human Rights Violations in Apartheid South Africa." *Social Science Record,* vol. 22 (Fall 1985), pp. 9–11.

Johnson, Sharon. "Physicians Alerted to Risks of Abuse." *The New York Times,* May 23, 1985, p. 21.

Kitano, Harry H. L. *Japanese Americans: The Evolution of a Subculture.* New York: Prentice-Hall, 1969, pp. 31–32, 42.

Kleg, Milton, and Marion J. Rice. *Race, Caste, and Prejudice: Handbook.* Athens, GA.: Anthropology Curriculum Project, 1970, pp. 44, 53–54.

Kleg, Milton, Marion J. Rice, and Wilfred Bailey. *Race, Caste, and Prejudice,* Athens, GA.: Anthropology Curriculum Project, 1970, pp. 25, 112, 122–23.

Lindop, Edmund. *Birth of the Constitution.* Hillside, NJ: Enslow Publishers, 1977.

Myrdal, Gunnar. *An American Dilemma: The Negro Problem and Modern Democracy.* New York: Harper & Row, 1944.

Pizzey, Erin. *Scream Quietly or the Neighbors Will Hear.* Hillside, NJ: Enslow Publishers, 1977.

Rauschning, Hermann. *The Voice of Destruction.* New York: Putnam, 1940. p. 232.

Washburn, Wilcomb E., ed. *The American Indian and the United States: A Documentary History.* New York: Random House, 1973, vols. I & II.

Chapter Four

Amnesty International USA. *Political Killings By Governments.* New York: Amnesty International USA, 1983.

Apple, R.W. "Iran's Bahá'ís: Some Call It Genocide." *The New York Times,* February 27, 1983.

Arens, Richard. *Genocide in Paraguay.* Philadelphia, PA: Temple University Press, 1976.

Baird, Jay W., ed. *From Nuremberg to My Lai.* Lexington, MA: D.C. Heath and Company, 1972.

Bardsajian, Kevork B. *Hitler and the Armenian Genocide.* Cambridge, MA: The Zoryan Institute, 1986.

Brown, Dee. *Bury My Heart at Wounded Knee: An Indian History of the American West.* New York: Holt, Rinehart, Winston, 1970.

Charny, Israel W. "Genocide: The Ultimate Human Rights Problem." *Social Education.* September 1985.

Charny, Israel W. *"How Can We Commit the Unthinkable?": Genocide: The Human Cancer.* Boulder, CO: Westview Press, 1984.

Charny, Israel W., ed. *Toward the Understanding and Prevention of Genocide.* Boulder, CO: Westview Press, 1984.

Chartock, R. and J. Spencer. *The Holocaust Years: Society on Trial.* New York: Bantam Books, 1978.

240

Fein, Helen. *Accounting for Genocide: Victims—and Survivors of the Holocaust.* New York: Free Press, 1979.

Hawk, David. "The Killing of Cambodia: Was It Genocide? A Report on Pol Pot's Brutalities." *New Republic.* Vol. 187, November 15, 1983, pp. 17–21.

Hovannisian, Richard G., ed. *The Armenian Genocide in Perspective.* New Brunswick, NJ: Transaction Press—Rutgers University, 1986.

Institute of the International Conference on the Holocaust & Genocide. *Internet on the Holocaust and Genocide.* Special Double Issue 3–4. January 1986.

Kloian, Richard D., ed. *The Armenian Genocide: News Accounts from the American Press, 1915– 1922.* Third edition. Berkeley, CA: AAC Books, 1985.

Kuper, Leo. *Genocide: Its Political Use in the Twentieth Century.* New Haven, CT: Yale University Press, 1981.

Kuper, Leo. *International Action Against Genocide, Minority Rights Group Report, No. 53.* London: Minority Rights Group, 1983.

Kuper, Leo. *The Prevention of Genocide.* New Haven, CT: Yale University Press, 1985,

Lang, David Marshall and Christopher J. Walker. *The Armenians, Minority Rights Group Report No. 32.* London: Minority Rights Group, 1981.

Lifton, Robert Jay. *The Nazis Doctors: Medical Killing and the Psychology of Genocide.* NY: Basic Books, 1986.

"Pol Pot's Lifeless Zombies." *Time,* December 3, 1979.

Rummel, R.S. "War Isn't This Century's Biggest Killer." *The Wall Street Journal,* July 7, 1986.

Shawcross, William. *The Quality of Mercy: Cambodia, Holocaust and Modern Conscience.* New York: Simon and Schuster, 1984.

Simpson, John and Janna Bennet. *The Disappeared and the Mothers of the Plaza: The Story of the 11,000 Argentinians Who Vanished.* New York: St. Martin's Press, 1985.

Totten, Samuel. "An Interview with Dr. Israel Charny, Co-Director of the Pilot Study on the Genocide Early Warning System." *Ecology Digest.* No. 9. Summer 1981.

Wiesel, Elie. *Night.* New York: Avon, 1967.

Wiesel, Elie. "Review of The Chronicle of the Lodz Ghetto, 1941–1944." The New York Times Book Review, April 19, 1984.

Zoryan Institute. *The Armenian Experience.* Genocide: Cambridge, MA: Zoryan Institute, 1984.

Chapter Five

Amnesty International. *Amnesty International 1986.* London: Amnesty International, 1986.

Amnesty International. *Prisoners of Conscience.* London: Amnesty International, 1981.

Amnesty International USA. *Conscience and Human Rights: An Amnesty International Curriculum.* San Francisco: Amnesty International USA, 1981.

Amnesty International USA. *Disappearances: A Workbook.* New York: Amnesty International USA, 1981.

Amnesty International USA. *Political Killings by Governments.* New York: Amnesty International USA, 1983.

Branson, Margaret Stimmann and Judith Torney-Purta. *International Human Rights, Society, and the Schools.* Washington, D.C.: National Council for the Social Studies, 1982.

Dobrin, Arthur, Lynn Dobrin, and Thomas F. Liotti. *Convictions: Political Prisoners—Their Stories.* Maryknoll, NY: Orbis Books, 1981.

Fireside, Harvey. *Soviet Psychoprisons.* NY: W.W. Norton & Company, 1979.

Lopez, Laura. "Torture: A Worldwide Epidemic." *Time,* April 16, 1984.

Ramirez, Antonio. "Political Prisoners: A Global Community." *Social Education,* September 1985, pp. 463–464.

Rubenstein, Joshua. *Soviet Dissidents: Their Struggles for Human Rights.* Boston: Beacon Press, 1980.

Schumacher, Edward. "An Age-Old (but Still Common) Horror." *The New York Times,* December 2, 1984, p. 4E.

Toronto Arts Group for Human Rights. *The Writer and Human Rights.* Garden City, NY: Anchor Press, 1983.

"Torture as Policy: The Network of Evil." *Time* (European Edition), August 16, 1976, p. 14.

Totten, Samuel. "Educating About and For International Human Rights." *Educational Leadership.* May 1986, pp. 60–64.

Wasserman, Harvey. "Amnesty International's Politics of the Heart." *New Age Journal.* October 1983, pp. 34–38, 90.

Chapter Six

"Jews Suffer Worst in Argentina's Prisons." *Jerusalem Post,* February 4, 1980.

Kinzer, Stephen. "Ex-Inmates Cite Harsh Managua Jail." *The New York Times,* August 24, 1986.

Lopez, Laura. "Torture: A Worldwide Epidemic." *Time,* April 16, 1984, p. 39.

McGrory, Mary. "Khomeini's Evil Theocracy." *The Sacramento Bee,* November 16, 1986.

Parry, L. A. *The History of Torture in England.* Montclair, NJ: Patterson Smith, 1975.

Perlez, Jane. "Jersey 'Town Meetings' Focus on Latin America." *The New York Times,* June 20, 1983.

Ramirez, Antonio. "Political Prisoners: A Global Community. *Social Education,* September 1985, p. 463.

Schumacher, Edward. "An Age-Old (but Still Common) Horror." *The New York Times,* December 2, 1984.

Stepan, Alfred. "Review of Nuca Mas: The Report of the Argentine National Commission on the Disappeared." *The New York Times Book Review,* November 23, 1986, p. 21.

"Torture as Policy: The Network of Evil." *Time* (European edition), August 16, 1976.

Chapter Seven

Alangir, Mohiuddin. *Famine in South Asia: Political Economy of Mass Starvation.* Cambridge: Oelgeschlager, Gunn, & Hain, 1980.

Blair, William G. "Study Finds Food Scarcities Rising Among the Poor of East Harlem." *The New York Times,* May 9, 1985, p. 10.

Bohr, Paul. *Famine in China and the Missionary.* Cambridge, MA: Harvard University Press, 1972. pp. 20–21.

Borgstrom, Georg. *The Hunger Planet: The Modern World at the Edge of Famine.* New York: Macmillan, 1972.

Brown, Lester, et. al. *State of the World.* Washington, D.C.: Worldwatch Institute, 1987.

Clark, Colin. *Starvation or Plenty.* New York: Taplinger, 1970.

U.S. Congress. House. *Problems of Hunger and Malnutrition: Hearing Before the Subcommittee on Domestic Marketing, Consumer Relations, and Nutrition.* Washington, D.C.: U.S. Government Printing Office, 1983.

Dando, William A. *The Geography of Famine.* New York: John Wiley, 1980.

Elfring, Chris. "Africa Tomorrow—If We Act Today." *BioScience,* vol. 35, no. 7 (July–August 1985), pp. 400–402, 407.

The End Hunger Network. *Mission Possible: The End of World Hunger by the Turn of the Century.* Los Angeles, CA: End World Hunger Network, 1985.

"Erosion, Drought and Deserts." *UNESCO Courier,* January 1985, p. 8.

Franke, Richard W., and Barbara H. Chasin. *Seeds of Famine: Ecological Desctruction and the Development Dilemma in West African Sahel.* Montclair, NJ: Allenheld, Osmun, 1980, p. 8

George, Susan. *How the Other Half Dies: The Real Reasons for World Hunger.* Montclair, NJ: Allanheld, Osmun, 1977.

Harris, Miles F. *Breakfast in Hell,* New York: Poseidon Press, 1986, p. 157.

Hartmann, Betsy, and James Boyce. *Needless Hunger: Voices from a Bangladesh Village.* San Francisco: Institute for Food and Development Policy, 1982, pp. 27, 37.

Hildebrand, George C., and Gareth Porter. *Cambodia: Starvation and Revolution.* New York: Monthly Review Press. p. 27.

Hollings, Ernest F. *The Case Against Hunger: A Demand for a National Policy.* New York: Cowles Book Co., 1970, p. 12.

Hooper, Ed. "Sudan: A Saudi Oasis." *The Middle East Internation,* June 28, 1985, pp. 10– 11.

Huebner, Albert. "World Hunger Myths. Taking Food from the Poor's Mouth." *Nation,* June 22, 1985, pp. 766–67.

Kahn, E. J., Jr. "Profiles: The Staffs of Life: The Future of the Planet." *The New Yorker,* March 11, 1985, pp. 50–85.

Lappé, Frances M., and Joseph Collins. *Died for a Small Planet.* New York: Ballantine, 1987.

Lappé, Frances M., and Joseph Collins. *World Hunger: Twelve Myths.* New York: Grove Press, 1986.

Lelyveld, Joseph. "Hunger in America." *The New York Times Magazine,* June 16, 1985, pp. 20– 23, 51–53, 59, 68.

Loveday, A. *The History and Economics of Indian Famines.* London: G. Bell & Sons, 1914, p. 11.

McCall, Cheryl. "Cry, the Pitiless Land." *Life,* May 1985, pp. 124–34.

McHugh, Roger J. "The Famine in Irish Oral Tradition." *The Great Famine: Studies in Irish History 1845–1852.* ed. R. D. Edwards and T. D. Williams. New York: New York University Press, 1957. pp. 434–35.

245

Mann, Judy. "An Expert on Hunger." *Washington Post,* November 1, 1985, p. 3C.

Meltzer, Milton. *Poverty in America.* New York: William Morrow, 1986, pp. 4–5.

Mooneyham, W. Stanley. *What Do You Say to a Hungry World? TX: Word Books,* 1975, p. 175.

Morris, Colin. *Include Me Out! Confessions of an Ecclesiastical Coward.* London: Epworth Press, 1968, pp. 39–41.

Murdoch, William V. *The Poverty of Nations: The Political Economy of Hunger and Population.* Baltimore: The Johns Hopkins University Press, 1980.

O'Brien, Patrick M. "Agricultural Productivity and the World Food Market." *Environment,* vol. 27, no. 9 (November 1985), pp. 14–20, 32–37.

Parker, Tom. "A Day in the Life." *Mother Jones,* February–March 1985, p. 10.

Parry, Martin, et al. "Climatic Change." *Environment.* January–February, 1985, pp. 4–5, 43.

"Peasant Rising." *Economist,* February 2, 1985, pp. 11–12.

Physician Task Force on Hunger in America. *Hunger in America: The Growing Epidemic.* Middletown, CT: Wesleyan University Press, 1985.

Raasch, Chuck. "Ethiopia's Agony: Starving Continues." *USA Today,* March 22, 1985, p. 5A.

Raloff, Janet. "Africa's Famine: The Human Dimension." *Science News,* May 11, 1985, p. 299.

Schwartz-Nobel, Loretta. *Starving in the Shadow of Plenty.* New York: G. P. Putnam's Sons, 1981, pp. 35–36.

Sterling, Claire. "The Making of the Sub-Saharan Wasteland." *Atlantic Monthly, May 1974,* p. 100.

The Hunger Project. *Ending Hunger: An Idea Whose Time Has Come.* New York: Praeger, 1985. pp. 396– 97.

Timberlake, Lloyd. *Africa in Crisis.* Washington, D.C.: International Institute for Environment and Development, 1986.

Trimble, Jeff. "Mozambique's Marxist Turn to the West." *U.S. News & World Report,* February 25, 1985, pp. 37–38.

UNICEF. *State of the World's Children.* New York: UNICEF, 1987.

Van Apeldoorn, G. J. *Perspectives on Drought and Famine in Nigeria.* London: George Allen & Unwin, 1981.

Watson, Russell, et al. "We Are the Children." *Newsweek,* June 3, 1985, pp. 28–34.

Watts, Michael. *Silent Violence: Food, Famine, and Peasantry in Northern Nigeria.* Berkeley: University of California Press, 1983.

Williams, Lynora. "Eritrea: Ethiopia's Famine Weapon." *Guardian,* May 29, 1985, pp. 9–10.

Willis, David K. "Drought Edges Toward the Nile." *Christian Science Monitor,* May 13, 1985, pp. 1, 14.

Chapter Eight

Amnesty International USA. "Good News and Words of Thanks." *Amnesty Action,* April 1984, p. 7.

———"When the First Two Hundred Letters Came . . ." New York: Amnesty International USA, 1982, p. 1.

Bloomfield, Lincoln P. "United Nations." *World Book.* New York: World Book, 1984, pp. 24–40f.

Power, Jonathan. *Amnesty International: The Human Rights Story.* New York: Pergamon Press, 1981.

Wasserman, Harvey. "Amnesty International's Politics of the Heart." *New Age Journal,* October 1983, pp. 34–38, 90.

Index

medical services, 81
Boas, Franz, 47, 48
Boston, 184
Brazil, 144, 155, 157–158,
    177–178
Bread for the World, 205
Brookline, Massachusetts, 214
Bureau of Indian Affairs, 72–73
Burke, Edmund, 91, 193, 215
Burkina, Faso, 192
Burundi, 218
Butler, Richard G., 49

C

Cambodia. *See* Kampuchea.
Cambodians in America, 58
Cameroon, 126
Catholic Church, 22, 139–140,
    155
Central America, 179
Chad, 170, 180–181, 183
Charny, Israel, 120
Cheyenne Indians, 30
Chief Joseph, 30
children, 11, 73, 95
Chile, 126, 130, 137, 146, 149
China, 126, 133, 138, 169, 189,
    218
Christian scholars, 19
Christianity, 20, 22, 125, 126,
    139–140
civil rights, 14, 24, 37, 38, 42,
    202–203
Civil Rights Act of 1964, 68
Collins, Joseph, 190
Colombia, 177, 179
colonies, 181–182
Coloureds (South Africa), 61,
    62, 65, 79–83
Confucius, 21
Convention Against Torture,
    153
Convention on the Elimination
    of All Forms of

Discrimination Against
    Women, 77
Convention on the Prevention
    and Punishment of the
    Crime of Genocide, 198
Costa Rica, 178
Covenant, The Sword, and the
    Arm of the Lord, The
    (CSA), 49, 56
Cuba, 133
cultural rights, 37, 39
culture, 51–52
Czechoslovakia, 126

D

Dachau, 17–18
de Cuellar, Javier Perez, 123
death camps, 104
death squads, 114
Declaration of Independence, 25
Declaration of the Rights of
    Man, 141
Declaration of the Rights of
    Man and Citizen, 35
Denmark, 110
discrimination, 40, 51, 60–63,
    66–89
    England, 87–88
    Japan, 86
    South Africa, 80–83
    Soviet Union, 83–85
    United States, 66–78
    against women, 75–77
disappearance. *See* kidnapping.
dissident, 128
drought. *See* famine.

E

Early Warning System, 120
East Germany, 11, 14, 133
East Harlem, 183
economic rights, 37–39, 42
Ecuador, 164

250

Inquisition, 139–140
International Convention on the
   Elimination of All Forms
   of Racial Discrimination,
   198
International Covenant on
   Economic, Social, and
   Cultural Rights, 40–45,
   198
International Covenant on Civil
   and Political Rights, 40–45
international companies,
   177–179, 182
International Red Cross, 196,
   211
Iran, 43, 88, 94–95, 133
isonomia, 19–20
isogoria, 20
Italy, 181

J
Japan, 65, 86–87, 180
Japanese Americans, 57
Jews, 36, 49, 50, 53, 54, 66, 67,
   72, 84–86, 88, 91, 95,
   101–111, 120, 126,
   142–143, 217
John, King of England, 22–23

K
Kampuchea, 113–115, 126, 164,
   213, 218
Kennedy, Edward M., 75
Kenya, 170, 211
Khmer Rouge, 115–116, 213
Khomeini, Ayatollah Ruhollah,
   59, 136, 219
kidnapping, 11, 132
King, Martin Luther, Jr., 9–10,
   69, 71
Koch, Edward, 69
Ku Klux Klan, 47, 49, 69, 71
Kuper, Leo, 118–119

kwashiorkor, 167

L
Lappé, Francis Moore, 190
Lemkin, Raphael, 91
Libya, 126, 200
Lippmann, Walter, 54
Locke, John, 25

M
Maddocks, Melvin, 9
Magna Carta, 22–23, 26
majority. *See* social majority.
malnutrition, 165–167, 186, 205
Mexico, 167
Middle Ages, 21–22, 93, 137,
   139
minority. *See* social minority.
Mormons, 56–57
Mozambique, 170
Muhammad, Elijah, 71, 72
Muhammad, Imam Warith
   Deen, 71
Muslims, 43

N
Nation of Islam, 72
National States' Rights Party, 49
Native American. *See* American
   Indian.
Nazis, 18, 36, 37, 43, 54, 91,
   101–111, 120, 179–180,
   217
New York City, 183, 214
Nez Percé Indians, 30, 33
Nigeria, 180, 218
Northern Ireland, 135, 155
Nuremberg, 120
Nuremberg Laws, 102
Nuremberg Trials, 110–111, 120

About the Authors

Samuel Totten is an assistant professor of secondary education at the University of Arkansas at Fayetteville. He was formerly a principal in California and has taught social studies and English at the secondary level in the United States, Israel, and Australia. He is a long-time member of Amnesty International and has worked with that organization in Australia, Nepal, and Israel.

Milton Kleg is currently a professor of social science education at the University of Colorado at Denver. He has also taught at universities in Illinois, Florida, and Israel. After serving in the U.S. Army, he taught public school and was a district supervisor. Dr. Kleg is the author of numerous works on terrorism, foreign intervention, and prejudice. He lives with his wife and five children and particularly enjoys the ancient board game called "go," the study of law, and shooting skeet.